Memoirs of a Southern Liberal

Robert Ayers

Bilbo Books Publishing
ATHENS, GEORGIA

MEMOIRS OF A SOUTHERN LIBERAL

Text Copyright © 2016 by Robert Ayers
Cover Design Copyright © 2016 by Kay S. Stanton
Book Design Copyright © 2016 by Kay S. Stanton

No part of this publication may be reproduced in whole or in any part, or stored in a retrieval system, or transmitted in any form or by any means, electronic, mechanical, photocopying, recording, or otherwise, without written permission of the publisher. For information regarding permission, write to

bilbobookspublishing@gmail.com

ISBN - 978-0-9800108-8-6
ISBN - 0-9800108-8-8

All rights reserved. Published in the United States of America by
Bilbo Book Publishers, Athens, Georgia.

www.bilbobooks.com

Dedicated to my children

Charles Jerry Ayers
and
Sandra Louise Ayers Holton

First Baptist Church in Forest City, North Carolina

PREFACE

As a PK, I had an early inkling that I might pursue a religious life myself, but I didn't know I'd become a liberal. I didn't know I'd morph from a smalltown uptown boy into an Ivy League-educated, controversial, reform-minded Baptist minister and later a nondenominational Professor of World Religions in a state university. I had no inkling how much anger I would create by merely trying to make this a better world. When I was just a wide-eyed son of a preacher in my North Carolina birthplace I had no idea that, forty-three years later, I would play a part in the largest change to happen to The South since 1865, integration. I was blissfully clueless that, a few decades down the road I would wind up riding around Athens, Georgia with a few other progressive and determined liberal UGA faculty members, protecting the first two African-American students at the University of Georgia from being beaten or murdered. Charlayne Hunter and Hamilton Holmes were pioneers, two brave teenagers wading into a mob of white resentment fueled by restrictive conservative ideology. We open-minded liberals wanted to prove to the world that even the Deep South could overcome decades of prejudice and segregation. In order to do that, we had to keep them alive. They were living every minute of every day under the very real threat of murder. Ignorance is not an easy enemy to defeat.

I must confess that these memoirs are highly selective. While I have made use of some materials from my files covering most of the years I have spent at the University of Georgia, I did not keep a journal during my lifetime, and therefore for the most part have had to depend on my memory for this account of certain conditions and events which occurred during my relatively long life, from February 24, 1918 to the present. This period of more than 90 years has been a time of momentous events (probably the same could be said of all ages in history) and of rather dramatic changes. It has included World War I and II, the Great Depression, the Korean and Vietnam conflicts, and the amazing technological developments in communications and other areas. In the South it has included the demise of "King Cotton" and the cotton mill, the rise of diversified agriculture and industry, a declining rural population, and the growth of great cities. Overall there appears to be greater economic prosperity, although large pockets of poverty remain. Churches profited from this economic development, as evidenced by the post World War II boom in the construction of new church buildings. Whether or not this has resulted in the growth and practical application of justice and Christian love in human relationships in both the personal and social spheres surely is an open question.

One of the most important developments in the South, the Civil Rights movement, largely was the product of the black church with most of the white churches either sitting on the sidelines or actively opposing the movement. In spite of all opposition, the Civil Rights movement produced great changes in the social structure of the South with the banishing of legal segregation from such areas as schools, public accommodations, and the work place. <u>So it is that the South of today is greatly different from the South of my youth.</u> The changes which brought about a different South in terms of improved economic and social conditions came as a result of great struggle and considerable sacrifice on the part of many people. While this narrative deals primarily with my personal life story, I do refer to some of these people with whom I was acquainted and the momentous events in which they participated.

As are all memoirs, so this narrative is determined by the events which occur during one's lifetimes, by one's station in life, and by the depth of investigation of the vagaries of one's personal memory. I have sought to be as accurate as possible in describing events in my past, but must acknowledge that some of them have dropped out of my memory bank, and that with the passage of time, past events now may appear to be better or worse than actually was the case.

In addition, it is surely the case that all memoirs necessarily are selective and colored by later experiences and developing patterns of thought. It seems rather obvious that everyone operates within some frame of reference or structure of meaning, whatever it may be. The events we experience are not just bare happenings, but are incorporated into some system of meaning.

An important question, then, is whether or not the frame of reference or structure of meaning provides an adequate foundation in light of which the facts of experience can make some sort of sense. Even though this principle of interpretation may not arise out of experience, can it stand the test of logical consistency in its explication and be applied to experience in meaningful ways? In my judgment, the acceptance of a God of unsurpassable love who desires that all human beings love Him and one another is a frame of reference which can make sense out of life. While it may not always be explicit or obvious in these memoirs, I have sought, throughout my life, to understand events and experiences in light of this frame of reference, and thus must acknowledge that, to some extent, it has influenced my perception of the past that I have sought to portray in these memoirs. It does not follow that such influence obscures the facts of experience. Actually, it may shed greater light on their meaning, and I hope, in some small way, these memoirs do just that.

CHAPTER ONE
INTRODUCTION AND EARLY YEARS

"Jesus didn't die FOR us. He died BECAUSE of us."

In all candor, I must affirm that I became, have been, and still am, a "liberal," at age ninety-eight, no matter how many today may sneer at such a label. It seems clear that while some of the sneering arises out of a different convictional stance, much of it is due to misunderstanding and/or ignorance.

Somewhere I read that the Greek philosopher Aristotle once asserted that happiness consists in the unimpeded exercise of our highest faculties. The ability to read, understand, and use language is among the highest human faculties, and it is tragic that so many people in the world today are illiterate. It is also tragic that this faculty, which constitutes so much of what it means to be human in terms of memory, anticipation, and interpersonal relationships, can be used in ways which intensify estrangement, hatred, and ethnic, religious, and political conflicts. Much of this is due to the natural ambiguity which infects all languages, but even more is due to the conscious manipulation and misuse of words and expressions for some supposed individual and/or group advantage, especially in politics and religion.

Today, there is perhaps no word more misused than the word "liberal." For many of those in the area of politics, economics, and religion who accept the designation of "conservative," especially the extremists, this word has taken on a pejorative connotation in their common usage. This is the case because little attention is given to the standard dictionary definition. It is simply assumed that the meaning of "liberal" contains the following defining characteristics: support of a big, regulatory, spendthrift, and welfare government, the advocacy of socialism in economics, the prohibition of religious practices in public institutions, and the acceptance of a total moral relativity. From this it follows that the "liberals" are suspect as to character, intelligence, and patriotism, and are the culprits with respect to what is wrong in the world.

It is easy to see that this pejorative connotation of the word and demonizing of liberals is not justified whenever one consults a standard dictionary of the English language, such as the *American Heritage Dictionary,* third edition. The defining characteristics of "liberal" and cognate terms stated in this dictionary are as follows: "not limited to or by established, traditional, orthodox, or authoritarian attitudes, views, or dogmas/ free from bigotry (A "bigot" is defined as one who is strongly and blindly partial to one's group, religion, race, or politics, and is intolerant of those who differ) favoring proposals for reform/open to new ideas for progress/ and tolerant of the ideas and behavior of others." Synonyms given for "liberal" are "broad-minded," "tolerant," "open-minded," and it is claimed that the central meaning shared by these adjectives is "having or showing an inclination to respect views and beliefs that differ from one's own."

In light of this definition, "liberal" primarily designates a certain type of attitude or spirit rather than a certain type of doctrine or belief. A doctrinaire liberal is a contradiction in terms. This does not mean that liberals are necessarily lacking commitments and convictions, but that they attempt to hold to and act on them in a non-prejudicial manner. Although not always successful in the attempt, they seek to display good will and respect for those with different convictions, but without the sanctioning of any views or actions which might be or become deletericus to others. They oppose, as best they can, such views and actions but in a peaceful or nonviolent manner, while at the same time seeking to persuade the proponents to change.

It is of some significance, I think, that our English word "liberal" is derived from the Latin, *artes liberales,* which means literally "arts befitting a freeman." In the Middle Ages the *artes liberales* contained studies comprising the trivium – grammar, rhetoric, logic and *quadrivium* – arithmetic, music, geometry, and astronomy. In modern times the term "liberal arts" has been expanded in its designation to include other academic disciplines, such as languages, literature, history (political, cultural, religious), comparative religions, art appreciation and history, philosophy and symbolic logic, higher mathematics, and the various so-called "pure" sciences. It is not accidental that these disciplines are labeled "liberal." Generally, knowledge in these areas produces results such as an appreciation of the great cultures of the world, with their myths, artifacts, histories, and great thinkers (philosophical and religious), a rejection of the absurd claims made in various revisionists' histories, the ability to think critically (which is based both on the principles of correct reasoning learned from logic and the demand for hard evidence learned in the sciences), and an awareness in general of the workings and regularities of nature and the long evolutionary development of its species. Such knowledge is a bulwark against misleading and/or false simplistic claims and slogans, provincial and/or ethnic narrowness of vision and sympathy, and authoritarian and dogmatic judgments and bigotry.

In addition, there are certain fundamental positive convictions which generally characterize liberalism. While there is an awareness of man's inhumanity to man and other creatures throughout history, of man's indeterminate possibility for evil, there is also a firm conviction that human nature is fundamentally good, capable of indeterminate possibility for good. From this it follows that on the one hand the dignity and autonomy of the individual must be respected and defended from <u>arbitrary</u> authority, that civil and political liberties are to be favored and supported, and that government by law with the consent of the governed should be instituted and protected throughout the world. On the other hand, if human beings have not only a capacity for evil but also an innate capacity for goodness and creativity, then governments have an inherent responsibility to create programs which assist the poor and the oppressed to escape the shackles of poverty, ignorance, and racism and to realize their full individual potentialities. Since human beings do have a capacity for evil, governments have the responsibility also to restrain criminal and oppressive activity of every kind, while at the same time seeking the best ways to prevent such activity and to reform the perpetrators. When Georgia's governor, Nathan Deal, refused free federal Medicaid money to help poor Georgians for purely political reasons, it reaffirmed my belief in the need for more liberal leaders.

The meaning of "liberal" is nowhere more clearly exemplified than in the field of religion, especially if one considers some of the very basic stark contrasts in attitudes and theological tenets between liberals and fundamentalists. In general, the fundamentalist emphasizes the plenary inspiration and inerrancy of Scripture (every statement is divinely inspired and infallible), the subjection of all to original sin due to the fall of Adam, the justice and punishments of God upon the wicked, all suffering as a result of the punishment for sins (original as well as actual), an eternal hell for those who are not saved, bliss for those who are, and the near end of this world in a divine apocalyptic event. Liberals either reject outright or radically reinterpret each of these propositions. <u>The Bible is not a divine information service, but a witness to the revelation of God in historical events.</u> The biblical myth of creation and the fall need not be taken literally, but may be taken seriously as a striking way of designating every person's dialectical nature of egoism and altruism. God's nature (as disclosed in the historical Jesus) is agape, self-giving love. It follows then that God does not directly will or desire the suffering or punishment of anyone, and will not send some cataclysmic events upon the world, but patiently will seek to lure everyone into the divine fellowship. Generally, liberalism's emphasis is upon God's loving concern for everyone and the divine goal of an ultimate universal fellowship. If there's anything I believe in enough to call it my creed, it is this, the Golden Rule.

To an extent, this discussion concerning the meaning of "liberal" already has indicated some elements in the climax of my life's story, some of the social and theological views which, over the years of experience and study, I have come to hold as non-negotiable tenets within my total convictional situation. I am well aware of the fact that, given my personal limitations, I do not always actualize the liberal ideals (such as logical thinking based on factual evidence, and impartiality and tolerance for all) in my everyday experience, but I do hold to these ideals and strive to realize them in actual practice. I intend these memoirs, at least in part, to narrate personal experiences which provided some of the causal conditions resulting in a "liberal" position, some of the events in which I engaged, and experiences which I had primarily as a result of being a "liberal."

As I look back on my early years in a rather small Southern community I am somewhat bemused by the fact that I came to hold "liberal" ideals. Superficially, one might be tempted to surmise that just the opposite would be the case, given the popular stereotypical view of the South often portrayed in the movies. Southern and liberal would seem to be a contradiction in terms. However, if one takes a more profound look at the Southern environment in which I grew up, one will find that it was not some sort of monolithic structure (predominantly rural with plantations and large farms), but, as with so much else in life, was made up of dialectical polarities and a considerable pluralism.

The social environment for most of my early life (I was born near the end of World War I) was a relatively small town of less than 10,000 people, located in the western part of the Piedmont area of North Carolina, not far from the mountains. While, historically, this area was one on which farming was the major occupation, it had never been one with grand plantations and multitudes of slaves. By the time of my youth, in the 1920s and 30s, it was mainly an industrial region of cotton mills. The mills attracted workers from the farms (most of whom were poverty-stricken tenant farmers) and impoverished folk of the nearby mountains (nearly all of whom were of pure Anglo-Saxon stock). The promise of "cash money" was a powerful incentive to these people to seek employment in the mills.

Unfortunately, the desire for "cash money" was seldom satisfied. Often the mills were built outside the city limits of the towns in order to escape municipal taxation. Many companies built small, cheap houses adjacent to the mills (most with no indoor plumbing), which were rented to the workers. This guaranteed a constant labor supply and, incidentally, a means of controlling the workers. Many of these companies also built and operated "company stores," where workers could secure goods on credit, often at inflated prices, against their next paycheck, creating a never-ending pattern of debt. In addition, churches and grammar schools were built in the mill villages with the encouragement and financial support of the mills. In some cases, the companies not only constructed the school buildings, but also employed the teachers (cf. Pope, Liston. *Millhands and Preachers,* Yale University Press, 1942, Chapter IV). Most children of workers dropped out of school in their early teens and went to work in the mills. Even though <u>both</u> parents worked (generally on different shifts, meaning the women often worked at night), the pay of the children was needed to help support the family. Very few students managed to continue their education at the regional or central high school in town.

This situation of geographical, economic, and cultural isolation brought about the emergence of distinct social groupings, or classes. I vividly recall that one of the mills in the vicinity of my hometown was located within the city limits, but that its village and company store were across the railroad tracks from the main business and residential area of the town. While the workers were not subject to legal segregation, as were the blacks, and some small measure of social mobility was possible, they did form a distinct class. For the most part, they did not attend "uptown" churches, the high school, or social functions of the town people and did not purchase much from uptown merchants. Instead, they worshipped in their own churches, traded in the company store, and had their own social functions.

Although the mill workers constituted the largest social class in the county where I grew up, there were still some farmers and tenant farmers (mainly growing cotton for the mills), who constituted a second distinct class, even though they had the opportunity for a bit more social mobility than the mill workers. At the top of the social pyramid were the uptown people, mill owners and managers, professional and commercial groups, schoolteachers, skilled artisans, and white-collar workers. In his study of Gaston County, North Carolina, Liston Pope found that in 1930 the white population was made up of 66% mill workers and their families, 16% farm families, and 18% uptowners (*Millhands and Preachers,* p.51). The county (Rutherford) which contained my hometown (Forest City) was located about 50 miles west of Gaston County, and I am reasonably sure that even though its total population was smaller, the percentages were roughly the same. The fact that there were at least five cotton mills and their corresponding villages in Rutherford County would support the conclusion that mill workers and their families were the largest group. I remember that in one case, in a rather large unincorporated mill village (appropriately named Spindale), there were two mills.

Even though they constituted the largest segment of the population, for the most part mill workers and their families were kept in such a state of dependency and ignorance that they lacked the necessary power on their own to bring about improvements in the rather deplorable conditions under which they were forced to work. I will have more to say about this in a later chapter, but will simply point out here that, during the time of my early years, there were no labor unions (the workers' rural and mountain background had produced an individualism which, when combined with the opposition of all community authorities and leaders, made collective labor action very difficult, if not impossible), little in the way of safety and sanitation regulations, poor wages, "lay-offs" in depressions, and practically every aspect of life controlled by the company. Even the few "enlightened" owners or superintendents who had some sympathy for the workers were nevertheless paternalistic in their relationship with them.

In addition to the three distinct classes in the white population, there was a fourth distinct class, namely blacks. The conditions under which they worked and lived were even worse than those of the mill workers. For example, where a bright child of a mill worker could enroll in the town high school, an equally bright black child could not. Segregation laws made social mobility impossible. Any freedom of movement and of association were greatly restricted. Blacks were denied equal opportunity for education, for employment, and for housing. They were forced to live in what amounted to segregated ghettos and to work at the most menial jobs -- those which even the poorest whites would not do. Only a few were able to become somewhat affluent economically (some funeral directors, ministers, and teachers), but this modest wealth was gained from their own people, and, no matter how intelligent and well-off they might be, they were still prohibited from voting, holding office, and from any genuine participation in the life of the larger community. While white mill workers might be regarded as inferior by, and felt inferior to, uptown folks, all blacks, however accomplished they may have been, were regarded by most whites as inferior to all white people. For the mill workers, blacks were one group to whom they could feel superior, and thus prejudice against blacks was generally very strong in the mill workers' communities.

During my childhood and early teens I was only dimly aware of this class structure. In the early '20s my father accepted an offer to become the minister of the First Baptist Church in Forest City. The offer had been attractive to him because the church definitely needed to build an educational building (He had inaugurated building programs in most of his pastorates), the promised salary was rather good for the times, and the church promised to build a new parsonage next to the church building. This parsonage was an unusually fine house of two stories with central heating (a coal-fired furnace and radiators), downstairs rooms of parlor, a dining room, a sun room, a kitchen and breakfast nook, a downstairs bedroom and bath, and four upstairs bedrooms and a bath. Across the front of the house was a large porch, at the west end of which was an adjoining porte-cochere. At the rear of the house, with doors leading to it from the kitchen and back hall, was a back porch, which in the early days housed the ice box. My father's position and income (though modest when compared with those of most other professional and business people), and the location and quality of our house automatically made us a part of the uptown class.

While I vaguely recall one occasion when sitting in our family car, parked at the curb in front of a store I had a fleeting sense of superiority to a couple of mill village children passing by on the sidewalk and dressed in their bib overalls, generally I had no sense of being a member of a privileged class. I suspect that being the son of a minister had something to do with this, since my peers would deride me for being a "preacher's kid." This derision often brought about a fleeting feeling of inferiority, and from this experience I gained some sense of what it would be like to be plagued with this feeling. Perhaps more importantly, my parents, though conservative, never made disparaging remarks about the other classes. They did not challenge the social structures of the times. For example, we had a black cook who always entered through the back door. Still, they were kind in their personal relations with persons of every class, and my home environment fostered a spirit of charity and good will for every individual, no matter his status in society.

It is the case, of course, that my friends and playmates, whether from modest means or of affluence, were of the uptown class. The backyard of the parsonage adjoined the rather large lot behind the church (used for Sunday parking), and this made a good area in which we could play various games. Even though mill village children sometimes walked through this yard, since it provided a shortcut to their homes across the tracks, I do not remember any of them stopping to participate in our games. The players were from nearby homes along Main Street.

Our grammar school was located in an uptown residential area in easy walking distance from most homes, and all of the pupils were from uptown families. There was no busing. We walked to school, generally with friends we met along the way. It was only when I reached high school (which, although located in town, was a regional school enrolling non-urban children who were bused to school) that I gained a few friends from families who were not of the uptown class. There was one with whom I became a very good friend, due in large part to our common interest in athletics. However, since our school was within our neighborhood and in easy walking distance, most of the rural children were bused home at the end of each school day, meaning that my peer group was mainly uptown. I am not stating this is something which one should be proud of, but merely a fact, which must be included in the story of my early life. It could easily have restricted my vision and sympathy. Fortunately for me, there were other factors (two of which I mentioned above) which prevented this "accident of birth" and social position from evolving into a persistent personal and class pride and prejudice.

I am not sure that I will ever come to the awareness of all of the causal conditions which led me to finally question some of the commonly-held values, attitudes, religious beliefs, and their resulting social practices, which existed in the community of my youth. I suspect that some experiences which stand out in my memory are to be included among these conditions and are worthy of mention in this account.

In addition to the influence of my parents as mentioned above, my position in the family structure probably contributed, too. I was the youngest of five children (four boys and a girl), with seven years separating me from the next youngest. My sister was positioned between that brother and the two older ones. My oldest and youngest brothers were rather "wild" and were considerable embarrassments to my parents. The oldest left home for "The West" when I was still a baby, and, during my youth, I had little knowledge of him. Considerably later, my youngest brother dropped out of college and also "Went West." The siblings with whom I was the closest were the middle brother, James, and my sister, Mary. Growing up, I greatly admired James for his accomplishments. He had managed a filling station during the summers in order to secure funds for college tuition. He made good grades in college at Wake Forest. He played on the football team. He finished medical school, and then began the practice of medicine. Among my earliest memories were wearing the Wake Forest freshman "rat" cap which James brought home for me when he came back for a Christmas holiday, and going to Greenville, South Carolina to watch him play football for Wake Forest against Furman. From him, as well as from my father, I gained a love for games and sports. More importantly, James provided me with a good example of the importance of education and hard work in achieving one's life goals.

Of all my siblings, my sister, Mary, had the greatest influence on me. I came to know her better than all of my brothers, thanks to her being at home with me when my brothers were all away at college or elsewhere. During her junior year at Meredith College she began to have serious problems with her vision, and it was discovered that she had an enlargement of the pituitary gland which pressed against the optic nerve, producing double vision. Over the course of about a decade, she had three very serious operations to remove the growth, but after a period it always returned. The last operation was unsuccessful, leaving her blind. She died shortly thereafter. My memories of her are of an extraordinary good and loving person who refused to feel sorry for herself. Indeed, she did some secretarial work in a downtown office in the interval between the operations. In light of her own experience she possessed empathy for those who suffered and/or were disadvantaged or underprivileged for whatever reason. She, then, provided for me a model of that goodness which embodies an at-

Mary Frances and her parents

titude of love and sympathy for everyone, including the underprivileged of society.

<u>One of the great lessons I gained from my sister and parents during my childhood was that there is no necessary connection between sin and suffering, but that, if not most, suffering is purely accidental, the result of chance and not of God's will.</u> My remembrance of my sister is of a thoroughly good person. Even as a child I was dimly aware that she did not deserve such suffering, and that God could not be good had he, for whatever reason, willed such suffering upon her.

I felt the same way about my parents, who, during my childhood and youth, had more than their share of troubles. They endured the worry and concern about my sister, the expense of the operations (They had to take her to a hospital and surgeon in Philadelphia), and the great depression in which my father was shorn of his savings. He cut his salary by over half in order to help the church meet its financial obligations. While my parents still hired a cook to give my mother time for church work and for caring for my sister, they had to rent one of our bedrooms to schoolteachers (authorized by the church's governing board) in order to make ends meet. Certainly they did not deserve such hardships from God or anyone else. Their financial trouble was the result of the sin and greed of others, and not of anything which they had done.

I think that growing older and having experiences of life such as those described above resulted in a considerable mellowing in perspectives and attitudes on the part of my parents. They became less doctrinaire, less concerned with maintaining every jot and title of doctrine, especially when such obstructed human relationships gave additional force to insensitivity and bigotry, and tended to intensify distress and misery. I recall three rather simple events which seem to illustrate this mellowing, and which certainly had some influence on the development of my attitudes.

In my young days all the members of a minister's family were expected to be in church for all of the services and practically all of the other types of meetings. On a regular basis we went to Sunday School, to the Morning Church Service, to the Evening Youth Meetings, to the Evening Church Services, and on Wednesday evenings to Prayer Meeting. The Prayer Meetings were rather informal services, with my father calling on various people to offer prayers. Time and again he would call upon one particular person, an elderly gentleman, to pray. He offered the same prayer every time, so much so that I could predict what he was going to say before he said it. One day (now I am not sure of my age at the time, but I was probably in my early teens, meaning that it was a while ago and sadly I don't remember the man's name) I asked my father why he continued to call on Mr. X when the prayers were repetitious, lacking in good style, and had a few implications of dubious theological worth. The gist of my father's answer was that a poorly-constructed but sincere prayer was more acceptable to God than an insincere one, even were it of great beauty, and that Mr. X was a thoroughly good person, a devout Christian loyal to the church and genuinely concerned about the welfare of others. A person of limited abilities, he was unable to express his loyalty in assuming any leadership roles. Calling upon him to offer his prayer at the Prayer Meeting at least gave him the opportunity to express his loyalty, to feel accepted in the fellowship of the congregation, and to gain a sense of personal worth.

  A second example is, on its face, somewhat superficial, but I think still illustrates the point I am making. I recall that one year (I was probably 12-14 years of age) my birthday fell on a Wednesday. During the day my parents had not made any mention of it, and I thought it had been forgotten. Before dinner that evening I had been in my room doing my homework and dressing for Prayer Meeting. When I came downstairs for dinner, I was greeted by several of my friends shouting, "Surprise! Happy Birthday!" My mother had arranged a surprise birthday dinner for me. My friends and I were served in the dining room; Mom and Dad ate in the breakfast room. Perhaps most surprising to me then was that I was excused from attending Prayer Meeting. Instead, my mother had purchased tickets for all of us to attend a movie showing at a local movie house which had only recently opened. I do not now recall what the movie was, but it may well have been a Western with a Tom Mix, a Bob Steele, or a Hoot Gibson. As far as I know, my father never raised an objection to this action of my mother's. It all seems rather innocuous today, but such was not the case in the 1920s and '30s, especially in small communities where there were folks who thought that movies were harmful and evil. For my mother to purchase tickets and permit me to miss Prayer Meeting in order to attend a movie, even on a special occasion, certainly demonstrated a mellower and more relaxed attitude with respect to discipline and practice. It indicated that her expressions of love in the form of special treats for loved ones took precedence over a strict regime of discipline, religious or otherwise, if the two conflicted. Discipline was important but not ultimate.

I have many fond memories of my father, such as his presence on the sidelines of the high school football games in which I played, our playing golf and horseshoes together, and his conducting the ceremony at my wedding. However, there is one, which stands out as illustrative of his mellowing. I do not recall his ever, in my presence at least, articulating the point that while doctrine and discipline are important and to be followed in most instances, they are not absolute. But, by the time of my youth, some of his actions exemplified this point, and the one which stands out in my memory and made me proud of him was the following.

In our relatively small community, there was only one taxi operator and owner. Until the depth of the Great Depression, his business was sufficient to support his rather large family. But then, as the Depression grew worse, his business became almost nonexistent, and he was unable to keep enough food on the table for his family (there were no food stamps and welfare). In this strained circumstance, he was attracted by the promise of considerable cash and yielded to the importuning of the nearby mountain bootleggers (it was the Prohibition era) to transport their product to the towns and cities of Western North Carolina. However, he was caught in the act by law enforcement officers in our area and brought before the judge of our district. It was at this point that my father, who was aware of the dire circumstances suffered by this man and his family and knew and liked him even though he was not a church member, got involved. I do not now remember all of the specific details, if I ever knew them. What I do know is that my father, even though he himself was a strong advocate of Prohibition, was instrumental in securing for him a suspended sentence with probation, was involved in gaining permission for him to retain a taxi license so his business could continue, and helped him secure other part-time work to supplement the meager income from the taxi business. I do know that my father told the judge, "Judge, if you free him into my custody, I'll take responsibility for him." Knowing that if he did not work his family would starve, my father secured the man a mill job. Another thing I do know is that from then on this man became one of the most loyal members of our church, standing in the vestibule of the church and greeting everyone who came to the service each and every Sunday morning.

Throughout the years, these memories, and others as well, have had a considerable influence in helping to shape my attitudes and perspectives.

I suspect that my father's financial difficulties and low income during most of my youth had some influence on my emerging outlook. While my family was not destitute, we had to be exceedingly frugal. I remember my embarrassment at having to wear bargain basement clothes to school. Even though I may have only been vaguely aware of it at the time, such as experience probably contributed to the development of at least a rudimentary sense of what it must be like to live in poverty and near poverty.

During my high school years there were other experiences, some of which confronted me with the dire consequences of poverty and some of which led to questions about a few of the entrenched social and religious mores and beliefs. Among them are two which remain rather prominent in my memory.

One of them concerns an event which occurred in our church. A staff member of the state Baptist Sunday School office was addressing a meeting of the entire congregation, and, in the course of his remarks stated, "Our methods are as sacred as our doctrines." Even though I was in my teens, I was so incensed by such a blatantly absurd remark that I stood up, interrupted his speech, and loudly proclaimed that there is nothing sacred about methods.

As I recall, the speaker did not respond to my remarks but, after a moment of silence, continued with his prepared remarks. After I sat down I glanced at my embarrassed father, who was sitting at the front, and it occurred to me that I would receive some rather strict discipline when we were in the privacy of our home. Much to my surprise, my father never mentioned the incident. I often wondered if, in fact, he agreed with my position, but simply could not sanction my interruption of a speech given by an adult.

A second outstanding memory concerns an event which involved the social and economic sphere.

When he began the practice of medicine, my brother James worked as the company doctor in a mining community in West Virginia. At the end of my junior year in high school, he persuaded the manager of the company store to hire me for the summer. I lived with James and his wife, Inez, in a rent-free house provided them by the company as part of the remuneration for his services. It was a typical company house with a hand-operated pump for bringing water into the kitchen, no bathroom, and an outhouse at the top of many wooden steps on a rather steep slope behind the main house. Needless to say, the living conditions were not as comfortable as those to which I was accustomed in the parsonage in Forest City. Yet we all coped with relatively good humor. I have described this house simply to indicate the very poor living conditions to which the miners and their families were subjected.

Even worse than the living conditions was the exploitation of the workers at the company store. This took place on two fronts. First, there were the workers employed in the store itself. The manager was lacking anything approaching human kindness and oppressed his employees by requiring them to work twelve to fourteen hours a day (in spite of Roosevelt's N.R.A.) in order to keep their jobs. Some of these employees were young people of high school age who had to work in order to help with their families' finances. If, in his view, they were late for work or left early, he would lay them off for several days, during which time they received no pay. I remember one young man about my age with whom I sought to have friendly conversations, but he was afraid to stop working even for a few minutes. Coffee breaks were unheard of, and lunch breaks were only thirty minutes. Even though I worked ten to eleven hours each day, this young man was always there when I arrived in the morning and remained after I left in the evening. He told me in one of our rare and hurried conversations that he had to keep the manager happy by working such long hours because his family depended on his income, and he could not afford to be laid off. I too experienced the manager's ire for "leaving work early." I had been employed for about three weeks when, on a Saturday, I left after ten hours in order to accompany James and Inez to a nearby town for a movie. On Monday, the manager informed me that I was laid off for two weeks because I had left early on Saturday. For me, that was the last straw, and I quit.

The second front of oppression by the mining company and the company store consisted of their method of paying wages and the prices of the goods in the company store. Similar to the cotton mill companies, from their very beginnings the mining companies paid new employees for the first two weeks of work only at the end of the fourth week. This insured that employees would always have to use the company store, securing the necessities of life on credit. Each company store had an office which issued scrip against the employee's next paycheck. During my period of employment, I observed a check made out to an employee in the amount of one cent!

The stores were general stores, selling all sorts of goods, including food, clothes, furniture, and fuel. Before I left, I made it a point to check the prices of many items, and then compared them with the prices of the same items in downtown stores at home. The prices in the company stores were from ten to fifty percent higher. This provided sufficient evidence to prove the truth of the refrain in the old song, "I sold my soul to the company store." Given such conditions, it is no wonder that the workers formed unions and were willing to follow John. L. Lewis.

Among the many other events of my childhood and youth there is one which stands out in my memory with great clarity. I have mentioned that my parents managed to employ a cook. She prepared all of our meals, coming early in the morning and staying until after the evening meal. I don't know how much she was paid, but given my parents' economic situation, I am sure that it was very little, yet she seldom missed a day of work. It was not that she was the stereotypical Southern black mammy as was so often portrayed in the movies. She was a relatively young woman who occasionally let her resentment for her impoverished situation shine through in her attitude and body language. She lived in a shack behind the big houses across Main Street from our house.

One summer evening after supper I was sitting on our front porch from which I could view not only the street in front of our house, but also the western part of the downtown area. Dusk had fallen, the streetlights had come on, and our cook, Ray, was on her way home after finishing her work. She had to cross the street in front of our house where there was no stop light to control traffic. I observed her as she looked carefully both ways, and, not seeing any cars, started across the street. She had just about reached the middle of the street when I heard a car at the edge of downtown accelerate at a very high rate of speed. It struck Ray before she could reach the other side. Fortunately, it was a glancing blow and not fatal, yet her wounds were serious, and when I reached her she was bleeding badly. I yelled for someone to call an ambulance, but, of course, no one did, and anyway it would not have transported a black, nor the county hospital have admitted her if it did. We were able to get our family doctor to treat her wounds.

In addition to the difficulty in getting medical treatment for Ray, there were two other incidents in this situation, which, as the British would say, caused "the penny to drop," and opened my eyes to the evils of segregation. The driver of the car was the young son of a "prominent" uptown family. Having stopped his car, he ran back to where Ray was sitting on the curb and began to chide and curse her for not looking before she crossed the street. Obviously, he was trying to place the blame on his victim, and, because she was black, felt no compunction about cursing her. Angrily, I interrupted him, proclaiming that I had seen what had happened and that he was at fault for speeding within the city limits. The argument between us became rather heated, almost to the point of coming to blows. However, my father, who by this time had arrived on the scene, was able to restrain us.

By this time a local policeman had arrived. In our small community everyone knew the driver of the car and his family. The policeman's first act was to ask the driver what had happened, and on this basis he was going to charge Ray with violation of the pedestrian traffic rule of jaywalking. I protested that I had seen the entire event, that Ray had looked both ways before beginning to cross the street, that the driver had accelerated rapidly, far beyond the speed limit, and that he was at fault and should be charged. With my father supporting my version of the incident, the policeman decided not to charge Ray, but neither did he charge the driver. He only advised him to be careful not to speed in the city limits.

For some time I had been aware of our segregated society in which blacks went to their own schools and churches and lived only in black communities. I was aware that they were not permitted to attend white schools and churches, live in white residential areas, eat in white restaurants, or to ride in the front seats of buses. But I had not been aware of the radically different standards of justice applied to blacks and whites or how much injustice blacks were subject to at the hands of whites, especially law enforcement officers. The experience with the policeman opened my eyes to that particular evil of segregation, and I began to question other aspects of segregation, such as the Jim Crow laws.

While the experiences mentioned above led me to question certain religious and social beliefs and practices, during my high school years I did not engage, for the most part (except for my outspoken critique of the state worker's statement), in radical criticism of or crusade against such beliefs or practices. I think I was a rather normal teenager. Although neither large nor fast, I did participate in sports and managed to make the teams in football, basketball, and baseball. Undoubtedly, the reason I made these teams was that we did not have an abundance of skilled players. Generally, in our high school league we lost more games than we won, especially in football.

We did play games, especially baseball. However, since this was the Depression era of the 1930s, we had little in the way of equipment. Our baseball was very old and had been taped several times. The only bat we could secure was an old broom handle. Still, we had some fierce contests and got plenty of exercise.

Another game we enjoyed was called mumbley peg. I don't think this game has survived the test of time, but it was quite popular then. There were even multiple versions of this game, some of which involved knives. We didn't use knives. We used a broom handle (the church cleaners inadvertently provided us with most of our toys, going through a lot of brooms cleaning the large church building). We created our own version of mumbley peg. A piece of plank wood about 12 inches long and 3-4 inches wide was driven into the ground until there were only 3 inches remaining above ground. We cut a piece of wood about 10 inches long from the broom handle with a sharp point at one end. The point was placed on the 3-inch plank. With the long broom handle we would strike this point such that the 10-inch handle would fly over and over in the air and we would try and hit it. The batter was given 4 tries to get a hit. After that, he was out. Even though we could not afford excellent equipment, we had fun with what we had.

More important for my development was the fact that we had a nucleus of outstanding teachers who gave us a good foundation for learning. They knew the subject matter (after retirement my history teacher taught history at a nearby junior college for a while), required homework, and graded strictly but fairly. There are three who stand out in my memory: my history, civics, and Latin teachers. These three gained my respect for the extent of their knowledge and for their genuine concern for students. I am still appreciative for their contribution to my intellectual development. For example, even though I did not keep up the study of Latin, in researching an article, years later, I was able to remember enough to catch the error some scholars had made in rendering a statement attributed to an early church father. In my view they deserve much of the credit for the fact that I did fairly well academically in college.

During my senior year in high school, the teacher in one of my courses required all of the students to prepare projects on what they thought would be their chosen occupations or professions. I recall doing a rather lengthy scrapbook on the ministry. Some of the materials came from my father's periodicals and some were copied from his books, but I did all the work. Needless to say, he was pleased that I had chosen the ministry as the topic. My teacher also rated it highly.

My opting for the ministry as a vocation played an important role in the selection of the college I would attend. It was in the depth of the Great Depression, but my father had been setting aside small amounts from his meager salary in order to help pay for my college expenses. My mother had sold some property she had inherited in order to help my brother, James, attend medical school with the understanding that, in turn, he would help me through college and seminary. In addition, I hoped to secure something in the way of scholarship funds and/or work at the school. I applied to two schools, Wake Forest College (which James had attended) and Furman University in Greenville, S.C. Wake Forest offered me only a small athletic scholarship which, given my limited athletic abilities, I did not accept. Furman had scholarships for students committed to the ministry and whose academic work had been above average. I was awarded one of these scholarships (much larger than the Wake Forest scholarship) and the promise of employment on the campus. So it was that I chose Furman.

Mary Frances Cooley and Bob Ayers

CHAPTER TWO

COLLEGE AND SEMINARY YEARS

"Searching out heresy seems to be a favorite pastime for many fundamentalists."

In the fall of 1935 I enrolled at Furman University, the campus of which, at that time was located almost in the heart of Greenville, S.C., within easy walking distance of the business district. Even though Furman was supposed to be coeducational, the girls were housed and had most of their classes in the buildings of the old Greenville Womens' College, across town from the men's campus. Some upper-class women were bused to some classes on the men's campus. It was only years later that an entirely new coeducational campus was built on the outskirts of the city. My college career was spent on the "old" males-only campus, which still contained a few of the original buildings. The chapel and one of the dormitories built at the founding of the university were still in use.

As I recall, all freshman (except scholarship athletes) were housed in this oldest dormitory, which was drab and uninviting. The rooms were small, contained two beds, two desks and chairs, and two wardrobes, and had no conveniences. There was a constant battle with insects, and in my case a mattress which contained bedbugs. It was changed only after I threatened to return home. For me, the only advantage of living in this dormitory was that it was next-door to the dining hall where I had a job as a waiter.

Having played football in high school, I thought I would try it at college, even though I had not been recruited. Several days on the practice field made it crystal clear that I could not compete with the scholarship athletes, and that I could not spend all afternoon practicing football, do my job waiting tables, and have any energy left to study at night. So I dropped out of football, and consequently had more hours and more energy for study.

My freshman year was rather uneventful as far as controversy concerning theology and social issues were concerned. I began a study of classical Greek, which continued throughout my college career. Even though I did not continue it after college, it had a profound influence on my thinking. Surely one cannot read Plato's account of Socrates' Apology without its influencing one to seek greater courage in the cause of justice and to strive for a more liberal spirit. Furthermore, the professor of Greek, Dr. Preston Epps, was a genuine humanist in the classical sense of that term, a truly learned man of humble and generous spirit, an inspiration to all of his students. We gained from him much more than some measure of ability to read classical Greek. The majority of us came to have a deep appreciation for some of the greatest persons, thinkers, and literature of Western culture, and this was reinforced by a study of Greek philosophy with the philosophy professor, Preston Warren. Eventually, I majored in both philosophy and Greek.

I remember one particular incident during my freshman year which occurred when I was performing my job as a waiter in the refectory. As luck would have it, I was assigned to two athletic training tables for football players. These two tables were occupied by the largest players, with the largest appetites, and it was almost impossible to keep food on their tables. The floor of the dining room was tile and slick when wet. On one occasion, when rounding the corner of a table, my foot hit a wet spot and I fell back but managed to hold the tray of dishes full of food so that nothing was spilled. The player next to me simply took the tray, filled his plate, and passed what was left to the person sitting next to him. As I recall there was some laughter, but no one expressed any concern about whether I was injured. They simply demanded that I get more food from the kitchen. This experience, and others of a similar nature, raised rudimentary doubts in my mind about the values associated with college athletics. These doubts became more fully developed before the end of my college career. Even though there were some exceptions, it became increasingly clear to me that the majority of athletes were recruited simply for their athletic ability, without much consideration for their academic qualification. Furthermore, it became obvious that intercollegiate athletics, especially football, were less and less student-controlled and oriented. Even though it would be many years later and at another institution, the quip of a football player that "if any more players are injured, they would have to give the game back to the students" was an apt description of the situation as early as my college career. Football was becoming more and more of a business, oriented to a special segment of the alumni who seemed little concerned with the academic status of the University. Yet with my classmates I attended the games and cheered for the Paladins.

One of the people at Furman who had considerable influence on the development of my thinking and attitudes was a student, Sam Allen. At the beginning of my sophomore year, I had moved out of the old dormitory and into the newer Geer Hall, and was privileged to room with Sam. An excellent student, Sam was a senior, and already accepted at Yale Divinity School. From this fact alone, it was obvious that he had rejected fundamentalism and sectarianism, in favor of a more liberal and ecumenical theology. In the many conversations we had, I found his arguments to be sensible, clear and persuasive, and I began to move in the direction of liberalism.

During this year, even though there were many conservative ministerial students enrolled, there were quite a few who agreed with a more liberal theological stance. If I remember correctly, it was during this year, because of Sam's influence and actions that, much to my surprise, I was elected president of the campus ministerial society. My tenure lasted only one semester, for the next fall a larger number of conservative ministerial students enrolled, and I was not reelected.

At the end of my sophomore year Sam graduated with honors, and the next fall entered Yale Divinity School. Two years later I went to Yale, and again roomed with Sam for a year.

The academic years of 1937-38 and 1938-39 were definitely eventful years. It was my good fortune to meet a young lady, Mary Frances Cooley, who consented to have dates with me. I was attracted to her not only because of her appearance and personality, but also because, given her Methodist religious heritage, she was not brainwashed with religious fundamentalism as were some Baptist young people, and thus held an outlook more congenial with my growing theological liberalism. She was able to sympathize with my distress at so many of the events, which were taking place at Furman. We came to love each other, and eventually, in the autumn of my last year (1941-42) at Yale Divinity School, were married.

Mary Frances Cooley

Before I get to the story of the first, though certainly not the last, time I experienced a fundamentalist inquisition, I need to tell you about meeting the love of my life, Mary Frances Cooley. I first saw my future wife at Furman. At the time, the school was located in a residential area of Greenville, South Carolina. The young ladies who lived in the area, whether in high school, college or beyond, were in the practice of hosting parties and inviting eligible Furman young men to attend. I received an invitation to one such soiree from the hostess, a female student I knew. When I arrived I saw a large group of my fellow students, all male, gathered around a tall, slender, extremely good-looking young lady, all vying for her attention, all trying to make a lasting impression on her. Naturally, I wanted to meet her, so I enlisted the help of the hostess, offering to help her with party preparation if she would introduce me to Mary Frances. Waiting until the right moment, I finally found a window of opportunity, and introduced myself. To my delight, I quickly discovered that she was as beautiful inside as she was outside. She turned out to be an open-minded, liberal, pacifist, Methodist, unburdened by the shackles of fundamentalism. We spent most of the night talking, and I offered to walk her home. I spent most of that walk working up the nerve to ask her out, which I finally did when we had reached her home. We made a date for the following Saturday night, and I floated back to my dorm on the campus.

There was a pretty good movie house in Greenville, where I escorted Mary Frances on our first official date. I vividly remember holding hands with her during the picture show. We continued to date, going to dinner, the movies, and listening to the radio. We even heard the famous Orson Wells "War of the Worlds" radio broadcast together. In case you're not old enough to remember that, many of Wells' listeners that night missed his introduction, in which he told us that what was to follow was fictional. Seriously, it scared a lot of people. Mary Frances and I knew that it was fake, but half of the Furman campus ran, frightened, out of their dorm rooms that night, convinced that the aliens had landed. We just laughed. It was one of the first of many, many shared happy memories to come.

During 1937-39 there were inquisitions and conflict at Furman. The conflict arose out of the fundamentalists' efforts to rid the campus of what they regarded as a heinous modernism (or liberalism) corrupting the youth. Fundamentalist students reported to fundamentalist members of the board of trustees and of the South Carolina Baptist Convention, which resulted in an authorized committee of powerful fundamentalists holding inquisition sessions on the campus with the goal of a purge of "unacceptable" faculty members.

I think it was the case that powerful denominational fundamentalists had long been suspicious of Furman's faculty, especially in certain areas, such as philosophy and some of the sciences. **Searching out heresy seems to be a favorite pastime for many fundamentalists.** Previously, Furman's faculty had managed to keep a low profile and had been shielded by the president. Dr. Ben Geer, a scholar of classical literature. But this was to change radically in the academic year of 1937-38.

It was at the beginning of this year that there came to the campus a scholar in the field of religion who became the focal point for the fundamentalists' assaults on the "modernists" in the faculty. Somehow Dr. Geer had encountered Dr. Herbert Gezork, a young scholar and refugee from Hitler's Germany, who was on a one-year visiting professorship at the Southern Baptist Seminary in Louisville, Kentucky. There was a vacancy in the religion department and Dr. Geer offered Dr. Gezork a two-year contract to teach at Furman.

Since Dr. Gezork had studied at distinguished German universities and earned a PhD from the University of Berlin, his academic credentials were preeminent. Not only was he a young man of superior learning, but also of superior teaching skills. He had an excellent command of English and a good sense of humor. With the exception of a few hardline fundamentalists, the students in his classes gave him the highest possible rating for his teaching. I had the good fortune of taking a course with him in each of the two semesters of my junior year, Comparative Religion and The Psychology of Religion.

As might be expected in light of his academic background, Dr. Gezork approach to these courses was based on objective scholarship, and he neither omitted relevant material nor prohibited relevant class discussion, even of sensitive issues. I recall that in the comparative religion course we read accounts in the scriptures of other religions about the supernatural and/or virgin birth of the founders of these religions. For example, Buddha was a preexistent heavenly being who, in connection with a prophetic dream of a queen, became her first-born when she was forty-five years old, and the virgin mother of Zoroaster was supernaturally "glorified" when she was a girl of fifteen. The discussion of these narratives led some students to raise questions about the accounts of Jesus' birth, which in turn led to a consideration of the data for and against the virgin birth of Jesus.

It was pointed out that both Matthew and Luke report the virgin birth, that it is incorporated in the Apostles Creed, and supported in Christian tradition and belief. However, some of the students argued that the data against was stronger than that for it. They referred to such evidence as its absence from the earliest New Testament writings (Letters of Paul and Gospel of Mark), the inconsistencies in the birth narratives in Matthew and Luke, and the fact that only Matthew and Luke contain the genealogies which surely are in conflict with the birth narratives of these Gospels. There was some speculation that the birth stories arose as a way of countering the charge of some first-century opponents of Christianity in their claim that Jesus was illegitimate. Needless to say, such arguments incensed the hardline fundamentalists for whom belief that Jesus was literally born of a virgin was the cornerstone of their type of high Christology, which was necessary for their substitutionary-satisfaction view of salvation. In their view, to deny that the virgin birth actually occurred was to deny the faith and to be guilty of heresy. Even though he had not stated his own position, they took the fact that Dr. Gezork permitted not only the pro but also the con arguments to be discussed in his class meant that either he rejected outright the historicity of the virgin birth or that he did not regard it as essential for the faith. In either case, this made him a heretic.

    As far as the fundamentalist students were concerned, fuel was added to the fire during Dr. Gezork's second semester course, The Psychology of Religion. At the beginning of the course brief consideration was given to the accounts in various schools of psychology concerning the origin of religion. These included theories such as religion as a quasi-pathological symptom of human neuroses, religion as a mechanism by which people project their infantile fixations on the universe in an attempt to reduce the anxiety arising from the threatening aspects of nature and to gain a sense of personal and community security. Some theories found the origin of religion in humanity's search for solutions to emotional problems, others in the semi-psychological sense of ultimate dependence. In these, and in similar theories, the origin of religion was solely a human affair without any reference to the Transcendent. Even though Dr. Gezork was highly critical of these views, a few of the stubborn hardline fundamentalists, whether from prejudice or intellectual incapacity, misunderstood and actually accused Dr. Gezork of advocating the very views he rejected.

    Another discussion we had in Psychology of Religion that incensed the fundamentalists concerned the nature and function of prayer. A high official of the Southern Baptist Sunday School Board came to one the largest congregations in Greenville as the guest preacher during a revival. The minister of this church was a staunch fundamentalist, and the South Carolina Baptist Convention had elected him a member of Furman's Board of Trustees. One of the guest preacher's sermons dealt with the value and efficacy of prayer. In it he recounted the story of his being drafted to fight in World War I, of how he and his wife had prayed that his life would be spared, of how, when fighting in the trenches, a bullet which came his way had been deflected by the New Testament in his breast pocket and his life was saved, and of how this was evidence that God had answered his prayer. A few of the students in Dr. Gezork's class had heard of this story and managed to introduce it into the class discussion. Some found it to be evidence of spiritual pride on the part of the preacher. Why should God spare him while permitting other equally righteous soldiers to be killed? Is the nature and function of prayer that of satisfying our own needs? Is it simply a means of getting God to do for us what we cannot or do not wish to do for ourselves so that he becomes a kind of cosmic "bell hop"? Is not this actually a perversion and corruption of genuine prayer, communion with God, instead of support of its value? In typical fashion, Dr. Gezork permitted the class discussion to range freely over the issue of prayer. The fundamentalists were outraged that he permitted statements of the guest preacher to be questioned or criticized, and erroneously concluded from this that he rejected all intercessory and petitionary prayer.

Armed with erroneous charges from the fundamentalists, powerful fundamentalists among South Carolina Baptist ministers, some of whom were members of Furman's Board of Trustees, launched a crusade against Professor Gezork. A committee from the Board came to the campus and held hearings, and I was one of the several students summoned to appear before the committee. As I recall, it was very much like an inquisition, a charge I leveled against the committee. **I asked them what had happened to the traditional Baptist support for freedom of interpretation.** They informed me that I was the one being questioned, and that it was disrespectful of me, a mere college student, to dare to question them. One committee member went so far as to threaten me with expulsion if I did not show more respect. Upon mature reflection, I regret having taken such a belligerent stance, for it probably did the Gezork cause more harm than good. At any rate, I did gain control of my emotions, and, in an attempt to set the record straight, answered questions put to me by members of the committee. I insisted that it could not be concluded from anything Dr. Gezork had said in class that he personally rejected the historicity of the virgin birth, accepted humanistic psychological theories concerning the origin of religion, or rejected the value of petitionary prayer. Unfortunately, my testimony, as well as those of the few other students who supported him, failed to impress the committee as much as the contrary testimony by the fundamentalist students, and the committee recommended to the Board of Trustees that his employment at Furman be terminated. He had a two-year contract, but the Trustees, even though they had to pay him for the second year, ended his teaching at the conclusion of his first year.

This episode with Dr. Gezork opened the floodgates of fundamentalist assaults on the administration and faculty. An unholy alliance of fundamentalist alumni with pro-football alumni put the pressure on the Trustees to force President Geer to resign. The fundamentalists opposed him because he had hired Dr. Gezork, and the pro-football crowd opposed him because he placed greater emphasis on academics than athletics, and they feared that he would cut the football budget in order to buy textbooks or more books for the library. President Geer did resign, and at the beginning of my senior year the Trustees appointed as president a Greenville lawyer who had absolutely no academic experience. He satisfied the fundamentalists by firing some "modernist" professors, with written notes in their mailboxes and without any hearings by the appropriate faculty committees. He satisfied the pro-football crowd and the fundamentalists (for some reason fundamentalists generally seemed to also be supporters of football) by giving greater financial support to the football program.

Early in the second semester of my senior year I accompanied two young faculty members and a minister friend of theirs to a theology conference at Duke University. The minister, Mack Goss, a young, liberal Baptist preacher from Westminster, South Carolina, drove the four of us to Durham in his late-model sedan. The faculty members were Wesner Fallow of the Psychology Department and Bill Keyes, freshman counselor and teacher (I don't recall his field). I don't remember why I was selected to make this trip, perhaps it was because they knew of my strong support for Dr. Gezork. Whatever the reason, I was delighted to go, and was tremendously impressed by their reaction to having just been fired by the new president. Instead of feeling depressed, they were both in high spirits, full of humorous quips and satirical comments about their plight and the overall situation at Furman.

I became increasingly aware that during this time Furman had a faculty as strong, if not stronger, than any college of comparable size in the nation. Evidence for this conclusion was twofold: First, Furman graduates were accepted for further study by the most renowned graduate schools in the country (For example-Sam Allen and I were accepted at Yale University), and Second, and of more importance, faculty who had been fired, or had left voluntarily, secured distinguished positions in prominent colleges or seminaries. Professors Gezork and Fallow went on to Andover Newton Theological Seminary, the former as professor of Christian Ethics and the latter as professor of Religious Education. Eventually, Dr. Gezork became the president of this seminary, Dr. Fallow became the Head of the Department of Religious Education, and Bill Keyes became the director of the Youth Division of the World Council of Churches. Both Professor Epps (Greek) and Professor Warren (Philosophy) resigned from Furman voluntarily, with Epps going to the University of North Carolina and Warren going to Bucknell University. A nucleus of such distinguished scholars and teachers would bring to any institution of higher learning a superior academic rating. Therefore, the witch-hunt by the fundamentalists was costly to Furman, but fortunately, only in the short run. Furman has long since recovered, built a new campus, gained its independence from the South Carolina Baptist Convention, and built up a faculty of distinguished scholars.

In May of 1939 I graduated from Furman with a Bachelor of Arts degree, Magna Cum Laude. My parents drove down from Forest City to witness the ceremony. They were pleased with my academic honors, but distressed that I had definitely decided to attend the nondenominational Yale University Divinity School (YDS), rather than the Southern Baptist Theological Seminary, my father's alma mater. I proclaimed vigorously that, given what had transpired at Furman, I was opposed to studying at any institution associated with the Baptist denomination. If I did not go to Yale I simply would not go to seminary. Reluctantly, my father accepted this decision, but later I think he became rather proud that I had gone to Yale. While certainly conservative, he was not fundamentalist, and we were able to discuss many theological issues.

I mentioned above that during my last two years at Furman I met and began to date Mary Frances Cooley. Mary Frances was a native of Greenville who, after high school, had worked in the office of a local business. If I remember correctly, it was at my graduation ceremony that my parents were introduced to Mary Frances and her parents. They accepted her just as her parents had already demonstrated their acceptance of me. They had invited me to share meals with them (her mother was a superior cook), had taken us on picnics, and, on one occasion, her father had taken us to Clemson for the annual Furman-Clemson football game. The summer after I graduated they invited me to spend some time with them at a mountain cottage they had rented for their vacation. During the years Mary Frances and I were apart, pursuing our studies (she went to college when I went to divinity school), we would spend time in each others' homes during vacations. The acceptance by our parents on both sides was so genuine and full that it gave us an additional sense of security in our love for each other and greater confidence that eventually we would marry. In the fall of 1939 I entered Yale Divinity School and Mary Frances went to Mary Washington College in Fredericksburg, Virginia, and later to Furman herself.

Since, to that point, the extent of my travels was limited to North and South Carolina, it was with considerable trepidation that I embarked on the trip to New Haven, Connecticut. Air travel had not as yet come into

Yale Divinity School

its own, and the major modes of commercial transportation were trains and buses. I went north by train, which meant overnight trips on a day coach and changing trains in Washington and New York. This was my first trip by train and it was into the "alien" world that hovered above the Mason-Dixon Line. I managed to change trains without losing any luggage and, exhausted, finally arrived in New Haven. However, my troubles were not over. To save money, I took the Whitney Avenue city bus from the station to Prospect Street. Given all the luggage I had to carry, this proved to be rather difficult on a crowded city bus, and it was definitely embarrassing to cause such considerable inconvenience for the other passengers.

My troubles didn't end there. From the bus stop on Whitney Avenue I had to climb an unusually steep hill to get to the divinity school. With several pieces of luggage, this was a formidable task. Added to this was my uneasiness as to whether I was even at the right location, for when I stopped and looked up, I saw a structure, which definitely didn't look like a divinity school. Finally arriving at the top of the hill, however, I discovered that I had approached from the rear of the school and had first viewed the circular back of the chapel.

    I arrived a few days before registration for the fall quarter, in order to get settled, and the campus appeared to be deserted. Eventually, I found the apartment of the caretaker, a crusty New Englander whose salty language was somewhat frightening to a Southerner who had grown up in minister's home. It was about dinnertime when I rang his doorbell, and there came this raspy voice from inside wanting to know what the "blazes" I wanted. Meekly, I responded that I was a new student and would like to secure the key to my assigned room. He did invite me in, gave me the key and the directions to the suite of rooms I was to share with Sam Allen, and informed me that it would be two days before meals would be served in the refectory. In spite of his earthy manner, I found the caretaker to be helpful, not only then but later on as well. He was considered a "character," but was well liked by the students, perhaps mainly because he was without pretension.

    Since he had a summer job, Sam did not arrive until registration day. After getting settled in my room of the suite, I was rather lonely and a bit homesick, so I took a walk around the campus and discovered that it was laid out very much like the University of Virginia. There were four dormitories or "houses" on each side of the quadrangle, with their fronts facing the "quad," and, at the east side in the center stood the chapel. On either side of the chapel were the refectory, common room, classrooms, offices, library, and gymnasium. The quadrangle faced Prospect Street, and at address 409 it was in the heart of a residential area which was considerably different from the rest of Yale University and the New Haven business district.

    Upon returning to my dormitory (Taylor House), I began to wonder where I would go for dinner. As I walked down the hall to our suite, I noticed that the door of the single room next to mine was open, and, hoping for some company, knocked on it. A young, black man came to the door, and after mutual introductions we learned that we were both first-year students. His name was Bill. I indicated that as soon as my suite-mate, Sam Allen, arrived, we could gain some guidance from him since he had already been there at the divinity school for two years. In the meantime, what were we going to do about dinner? The dining hall was not yet open. He responded that he had arrived the previous day, had explored New Haven, and knew of a good restaurant. He would be pleased to have me accompany him to this restaurant if I so desired. Gladly, I accepted his invitation, and not only did we have dinner together, but also went to one of the downtown movies. For a white Southerner, who believed ideologically in the equality of the races but had never had the opportunity in the social sphere for a free and equal association with a black person, this was exhilarating. I could hardly believe that this had taken place on my first day at Yale, and it reinforced my conviction that I had made the right choice of seminary. I regret to say that while Bill and I were friends during our seminary days (I helped him get elected president of the senior class), after graduation we found employment in widely separated parts of the country and lost touch with each other. Yet I will never forget his kindness to me on my lonely first night at Yale Divinity School.

My first year at Yale proved to be not only exhilarating but also humbling. So many of the students enrolled in the three-year Bachelor of Divinity program (since renamed Master of Divinity) had done their undergraduate work at prestigious schools and seemed so self-assured with respect to their knowledge and intellectual ability. Then, too, among the students enrolled were those working toward their Ph.D. degrees in various areas of religious studies. In their company I found it difficult to avoid feeling inferior, but association with my good friend and suite mate, Sam, provided me with a sense of acceptance and self-confidence. Soon I discovered that discussions with fellow students, and especially with Sam, were stimulating my thinking and broadening my horizons.

As I recall, we were not content simply to engage in armchair conversations concerning Christian theology and the application of Christian ethics to social problems, but, on occasion, participated in causes for social reform. At the time, the state of Connecticut had a law on its books prohibiting the sale of and distribution of information about birth control devices, and some of us participated in a public protest rally advocating the abolition of the law. On another occasion, we participated in picketing a New Haven business establishment engaged in unfair labor practices. We invited social activists to come to the campus and speak to us in the common room about their activities for social reform. Among them were a few reformers from the South who spoke about their efforts and the difficulties they encountered in seeking to improve the lot of Southern agricultural workers and blacks. Of course, much of what we learned in some of our courses also increased our concern for social justice.

Fulfilling the requirements of our work scholarships and of our studies, and engaging in some social action, occupied most of our time. However, we did manage to find time for some recreation. We played handball in the school gymnasium once or twice a week, a game at which I was fairly good, winning about as often as I lost. This was not the case with respect to tennis. A tennis tournament had been arranged by the student council and I made the mistake of entering it under the assumption that my informal game could match that of any Divinity student. It turned out that I couldn't win a single point against my very first opponent. I didn't even return a serve or make a second shot when I was serving. Later, I learned that he had been an all-S.E.C. football and tennis player at Vanderbilt.

At the end of the 1939-1940 academic year, Sam graduated and became the minister of the First Baptist Church of Buford, South Carolina. Some years later, Mary Frances and I visited with him in Buford over a weekend. Still later, Sam moved to the pastorate of the Baptist Church in Manhattan, Kansas, affiliated with the American Baptist Convention. After that, we lost touch with each other, but I still have vivid memories of the time we spent together my first year at Yale.

I have written of the intellectual stimulation gained from conversations with fellow students. Needless to say, the faculty and the courses I took made an even greater contribution to my intellectual development. I stood in awe of these world-renowned scholars and found their courses to be on such a level of difficulty that, during my first year, I had to struggle to maintain a decent grade point average of B. My academic work improved somewhat during my last two years.

While all of the faculty were excellent scholars and most were superior teachers, among my favorites were H. Richard Neibuhr, Professor of Christian Ethics, Liston Pope, Professor of Social Ethics, Roland Bainton, Professor of European Church History, Halford Luccock, Professor of Homiletics, and Douglas Clyde Macintosh, Professor of Systematic Theology. One of my great regrets is that I was unable to schedule a course with the great scholar in the history of Christian thought, Robert L. Calhoun. I was able to secure a transcript of his lectures, a volume I still use and prize highly, and I was able to sit in on some of his classes. He amazed me with his erudition and his memory. Without any notes, he was able to quote entire passages from ancient documents and creeds, sometimes in the original Greek or Latin.

During my second year I was required to take three terms (the quarter system was in effect) of Macintosh's "Systematic Theology." As evidenced by the titles of two of his books, T*he Reasonableness of Christianity and Theology as an Empirical Science*, his theology was in the tradition of the "classical" theological liberalism espoused by such nineteenth century German theologians as Albrecht Ritschl and Adolf von Harnack. This is not to say that it was identical with these theologies, but that even though an original thinker, his thought processes has been influenced to some extent by them. He definitely argued that theology could be grounded in a critical monastic philosophical realism which affirms that the objects of experience, including the object of religious experience, actually exist independent of the experience, and which makes use of the tools of scientific method such as observation and experiment, generalization and theoretical explanation such that a body of empirically verifiable theological laws is established. Among other things, this places emphasis upon religious experience and the knowledge of God through the self's experience of moral transformation. Reason is more than simply harmonious with and a servant of revelation. Instead it functions as the source of revelation. Similar to the German liberal theologians for whom Jesus is the superb master in the art of living (Harnack) or the highest example of moral valuation (Ritschl), Macintosh held that the life and work of Jesus represent the highest instances of the human experience of God, of the right religious adjustment. The testimony of the Bible (analyzed by critical scholarship) and especially the life of Jesus are important sources of religious data, but through the use of critical reason applied to human experience such data may be found elsewhere (in other religions, for example). So the life and work of Jesus do not provide a <u>special</u> revelation of God, but are illustrative of principles, which can be discovered on grounds which are independent of the Christian tradition.

While I appreciated Macintosh's philosophical realism and his basic premise that Christian theology should be relevant to the modern worldview, it seemed to me that relevance did not necessarily require abandoning the notion of a special revelation of God in Jesus Christ. I was and am convinced that the disclosure of God in Jesus Christ was from above and was conclusive. Furthermore, in light of some beginning and rather small general acquaintance with the so-called Neo-Orthodox theology, especially as it was propounded in America by such theologians as Richard and Reinhold Niebuhr, it seemed to me that Macintosh held an overly optimistic view of the capacity of the human faculty of reason to gain a <u>full</u> knowledge of God and of what is required for a right religious adjustment solely on the basis of what is available to human experience as such. Given this, and the fact that Professor Macintosh's arguments were rather abstract and delivered in such a mild and soft voice that I had difficulty following his lectures, I had to struggle to earn average grades in the three terms of his Systematic Theology.

In spite of my disagreement with some of his theology, I held Professor Macintosh in high esteem. He was genuinely interested in students, inviting groups of students to social gatherings in his home. (His was one of only two faculty homes I visited.) During my time at Yale he was nearing retirement, having taught there for better than thirty years. A native of Canada, he had graduated from McMaster University and earned the Ph.D. from the University of Chicago. He began his career at Yale in 1909. Soon after gaining tenure, he sought to become an American citizen. Even though he had not opposed America's entry in to WWI, he found that he could not, as the application for citizenship required, swear to defend the United States under any and all circumstances. His first loyalty was to God, and it was conceivable that sometime in the future the government of the U.S. might enter into an unjust war, abhorrent to God. (I wonder what he would have thought of Vietnam.) His case was taken all the way to the Supreme Court, which ruled against him by a five to four vote, possibly due to the pressure of the country's involvement in the First World War. During the war he drove a Red Cross ambulance in France. Even though he spent his entire career in this country at Yale Divinity School, he was never able to become a United States citizen.

Whenever I recall my academic experiences at Yale Divinity School, there are two courses that stand out as having had the greatest influence on the development of my thinking and attitudes. One was Professor Liston Pope's two-term Social Ethics. The other was Professor H. Richard Niebuhr's three-term Christian Ethics. Even after fifty years I still possess the notes I transcribed in these courses. In these memoirs I cannot adequately describe their copious content, but only indicate very briefly the general nature and purpose of each course and a salient point or two from each.

As might be expected from the title, Professor Pope's course dealt with the issue of what is good for and thus what ought to be in society. Among other things, this included an analysis of Western Culture and a consideration of some philosophical ethics, but primarily an explication of the Christian faith's implication for and application to such social issues as: race relations, overpopulation, unemployment, workers' conditions, organized labor and management, the conditions of sharecroppers, juvenile delinquency, etc. Various responses to these issues in the modern history of Christianity (including fundamentalism, liberalism, European Neo-Orthodoxy, and American Christian Realism) were analyzed. I found that the approach taken in Reinhold Niebuhr's Christian Realism was the most satisfying.

He rejected the obscurantism and extreme individualism of fundamentalism, the naïve optimism of liberalism with respect to achieving The Kingdom of God on Earth, and the ethical situationalism of some Neo-Orthodox theologians. Given the self-righteousness of collective egoisms (such as nations and corporations) there are no simple solutions to the social evils which plague mankind and the three positions mentioned above are inadequate. The first two follow what might be called the "domino" approach. **Fundamentalists think that the saving of individual "souls" will automatically solve social problems, while liberals hope to eradicate social evils by persuading people to follow the path of love.** Situationalism is inadequate because it ignores the "middle principles," claiming that ethical decisions require only an analysis of the situation and of how to apply the closest possible approximation of *agape* (love) to the situation. But in this view, each ethical decision is made *ad hoc,* without any guidance from the ethical wisdom of the race, especially of Western Culture.

By contrast, Niebuhr's view might be designated "contextualism." That is, three factors need to be taken into account in the making of ethical decisions, especially with respect to social issues. They are the situation, the absolute norm of *agape* (the sacrificial love of God as disclosed in Jesus Christ), and what he called middle principles, which are a legacy of classical philosophical ethics and include such moral virtues as integrity, justice, equality, temperance, and peacefulness. In this imperfect world, this world of individual and collective egoisms, the full actualization of the absolute norm of *agape* is impossible in practice. The middle principles serve as its instruments, and their actualization generally achieves the closest possible approximation to agape. Yet *agape* is relevant to social problems as the ultimate and absolute norm which stands in judgment over all actualizations of the middle principles. It prompts humility concerning any achievements and reminds us of the relative status of the middle principles. Furthermore, it is relevant to social problems as the motivating force inspiring Christians to engage in the struggle for social justice. The means of securing social justice are the dialectic of persuasion and compulsion, but under *agape*, compulsion is non-violent.

My major project in the Social Ethics course was a study of textile unions in Greenville, SC. There were several reasons why I decided to undertake such a study. I had been inspired by reading Professor Pope's book *Millhands and Preachers,* a study of the situation in Gaston Country, North Carolina. Then, too, I had been aware of the plight of the mill workers in my own hometown (see Chapter One). Last, but not least, was the fact that Greenville was probably the largest textile center in the world, with 28 plants employing 17,000 workers, and that I planned to spend an extended spring vacation period there in the home of Mary Frances (we had officially gotten engaged the previous Christmas—when I had given her a ring). This would give me the opportunity to interview a considerable number of persons such as workers, union organizers, managers, owners or members of the mills' boards of directors, ministers, and educators. On the basis of information obtained from various written sources and from my interviews, I wrote a 35-page paper for the course.

The experiences involved in doing this study provided evidence supporting the soundness of Reinhold Niebuhr's Christian Ethics and his recommended dialectical strategy for dealing with social problems. It soon became obvious to me that, for years, the mill workers had been at the mercy of the owners and superintendents with respect to wages, working conditions, living conditions, and the charges for goods at the company store (that tied them, inextricably to a life-long system of wage slavery). The owners and superintendents were a dominant force in the power establishment in Greenville. In a very real sense, they weren't merely the bosses. **They WERE the economy, the education, the religion, the government, and the media.** The only thing that scared them was the possibility of unionization. <u>Even the ministers, who should have been concerned with the plight of the workers and should have sought to persuade the owners to improve the conditions, were, with one exception, in tacit agreement with the owners.</u> The "uptown" ministers were silent about mill workers' conditions and labor unions. Independent evangelists and ministers of churches in mill villages preached AGAINST unions, calling them the agents of the devil and communist-inspired company-wreckers. Without recognizing its implication, one minister told me that when the workers in his mill tried to organize, he preached that Christians should belong to no other organization than The Church. The fact that the mill owner gave him $50 a week might have factored into his thinking. So it was that some compulsion was necessary (organizing, the threat of strikes, appeals to the National Labor Relations Board) in order to bring about improved conditions for the workers.

Yet persuasion still had its role to play. The leading union organizer was a former minister who was well liked by all of the parties and sought to bring about change through persuasion. This "uptown" Presbyterian exception to the rule was asked by the largest local TWUA (Textile Workers Union of America) union in Greenville to serve as arbitrator and mediator for disputes. He arbitrated by persuasion and sometimes compulsion.

My Greenville mill life case study provided evidence in support of the conclusion that the philosophies of BOTH the moral cynics, who think that only coercion, generally violent coercion, can settle disputes, and the liberals, who think that appeals to good will and the "better angels of our nature" will win the day, were inadequate. They weren't separate. They were both needed. Both nonviolent coercion and persuasive appeals are needed to solve society's problems.

While Professor Pope's course in Social Ethics dealt with only the problems of society, Professor H. Richard Niebuhr's three-term Christian Ethics course was much broader. He defined "ethics" as moral reflection on the basis of first principles. This definition entails striving for clarity about moral principles and applying them to life's issues. Christian ethics is moral reflection and self-criticism by the Christian community. The task of Christian ethics is to bring moral reflection as much consistency and coherence as possible (and ministers are supposed to light this torch and lead the way).

In order to delineate the principles of Christian moral reflection, Niebuhr engaged in a rather lengthy analysis of the Biblical perspectives found in the Old Testament (especially the prophets), in the teachings of Jesus, of Paul, of other New Testament writers, and of the theologies of various other thinkers in the history of Christendom. Some of this analysis was structured in terms of certain TYPES of Christian ethics, such as:

1) The <u>new law</u> type, exemplified by Tolstoy and the monastics

2) The <u>dialectic</u> type, such as that of St. Augustine

3) The <u>synthetic</u> type, like Thomas Aquinas

4) The <u>dualistic</u> type, personified best by Martin Luther,and

5) The <u>cultural</u> or <u>assimilative</u> type, like that of Adolf von Harnack,

H. Richard Niebuhr's lectures were later incorporated into his excellent book, *Christ and Culture*.

My major project for this course was a critical study of two great Russian thinkers, Tolstoy and Dostoevsky. Tolstoy, after his "conversion," fit the (1) <u>New Law</u> type. The Sermon on the Mount was the new law which, given man's propensity for the reasonable, made it possible for each person to follow perfectly in all of the situations of life. If we all did this, Earth would be a utopia. This was a clearly moralistic view of sin and salvation, as old as the "Letter of James" in the New Testament and in Pelagius, Augustine's opponent. Sin was understood as certain acts, but, inspired by the good example of Jesus, one could at any time turn away from these acts and do good deeds.

Dostoevsky's view was somewhat similar to the dialectical perspective of Augustine, for whom sin is fundamentally an irrational and willful egocentrism, the attempt to usurp the deity, and is present even in the doing of good deeds. Salvation is a matter of humbly accepting the grace of God, that God lovingly accepts one even though he is unacceptable. In his novels, Dostoevsky plumbed the dark depths of the human soul, uncovering the addiction to unreasonableness and lawless freedom. Paradoxically, in his theory, lawless freedom results in the loss of freedom. Only in freely accepting the love of Christ can there be genuine freedom.

My conclusion was that, although there was much to admire in Tolstoy (his repudiation of capital punishment and of war), Dostoevsky's thought process was more realistic and profound, especially his understanding of human nature and of freedom. Further, the <u>dialectical</u> view of sin and salvation was more realistic, and more in harmony with the basic Christian gospel, than the <u>new law</u> view.

Mary Frances and I were married just before the fall term of my last year at Yale, on September 4th, 1941, with my father performing the ceremony. It was only with the continued financial support of both of our parents, my University scholarship, the limited funds from the church where I worked, and what money I earned at my summer job, that we were able to marry prior to my being graduated and securing a full-time position. Housing looked like it was going to be a problem, but we were able to secure an attic apartment in a widow's house on Winchester Avenue a few blocks down the hill from the campus.

Mary Frances and Sandra (the bride)

Yale let student spouses audit classes for free, even if they weren't enrolled. Mary Frances took full advantage, taking Christian Ethics, Church History, and Care of the Parish classes, in preparation for her later role as a minister's wife. We didn't have a car. We had to walk up the hill, through the snow, to class. Remember, we were both Southerners, not accustomed to snow.

Even while in divinity school, I worked at a church. At the beginning of my second year, I secured a position at the First Baptist Church in Waterbury, Connecticut. This job included teaching religion to Junior High school children in a "released-time program" once a week. It wasn't easy. The children were let out of the last period of their school day from a nearby public school. They came to the basement of the church and were hardly in the mood to listen to some young preacher-to-be. I wasn't a good enough teacher to do much good there and was constantly frustrated by what I regarded as my own inadequacy. I was, and still am, convinced that objective teaching of religion in public schools works better than a released-time program.

My other duties as a student assistant included working with the youth at church, especially in the Sunday School and Sunday evening youth groups, and sometimes assisting the minister in the worship service. I liked it. For one thing, the content of the program materials for youth provided by the American Baptist Convention (Northern Baptist) was thoughtful and progressive, theologically and socially. Dr. David P. Gaines, the minister, was a good sermonizer and minister.

The Sunday evening service was an open forum. After a brief worship period, members of the congregation were invited to raise questions about anything Dr. Gaines said in his sermon, or whenever. **I had never before encountered a minister who was so willing to be questioned by his congregation.** (That's just not how it's usually done in the Southern Baptist tradition.) In addition, he was both an able administrator and an accomplished scholar, having published an excellent study of the ecumenical movement.

Much to my surprise, I soon learned that Dr. Gaines was the brother of my high school history teacher, Mrs. Broadus Moore. It's a small world after all. Both siblings were thoughtful and superior people.

Finally, the many good people in the congregation made my work pleasant and made me, and Mary Frances when she joined me there, feel welcome. They did the little things. Every Sunday we were invited to someone's home for Sunday dinner. The church (Baptist, you recall) even voted to accept Mary Frances for membership despite her having been raised Methodist. They didn't even feel the need to rebaptize her with immersion (We dunk people all the way in the Baptist Church, north or South). <u>At that time, most Southern Baptists churches had requirements that new members be rebaptized, but, generally, the American Baptist Convention thought it inappropriate and an example of spiritual pride and sectarian prejudice to question the validity of other Protestant denominations' modes of baptism.</u>

In the summers of 1940 and 1941, in between sessions of study at Yale, I worked at my second church as a student minister (still not yet ordained, but licensed to preach) in a small community church in an isolated area in the Berkshire mountains, not far from Great Barrington, Massachusetts. Each church is quite different (especially in the notoriously independent Baptist denomination). The Berkshire church was a whole different world from the Waterbury church or from my father's church in North Carolina. It was a challenge, to say the least.

The population there was divided between permanent residents and the more affluent summer vacationists who owned or rented cottages or rooms in the guest houses. I soon discovered that there were some superficial boundaries between these two groups (especially among the young people), I sought to remove these walls. I tried to use games and the theatre, activities that young people from across the social spectrum all usually enjoy. I led them in rehearsals and the production for the congregation audience. They did all of this together, mixed, intertwined. I don't know whether or not this had any lasting effect on the lives of those young people, but for those brief summer months at least, they did all seem to gain some sense of community.

My experiences during those summer months weren't all pleasant. I was given room and board in the home of a retired veterinarian who, years earlier, had built an annex to his large farmhouse in order to take in summer guests. There were several paying guests, among them a number of affluent elderly widows from New York. They were all white Protestants (WASPS) who often gave vociferous expression to their anti-Semitic prejudices in the conversations we had over meals. Sometimes they went so far as to actually praise Hitler for his persecution of Jews. I reminded them that Jesus Christ was a Jew, but they rejected this out of hand. They'd counter with some version of Christ not being Jewish and God having even rejected the Jews. Their shady knowledge of God's plan aside, they were convinced, by virtue of their own race and religion, that they knew precisely what God thought and wanted. Apparently He didn't want his own chosen people. Reason with them as I might, I couldn't make a dent in their anti-Semitism.

Of course, they didn't limit their hatred to Jewish people. They also hated the inhabitants of New York's slums (mostly poor blacks and Latin Americans). These people, they claimed, did not bathe, and instead stored coal for their stoves in their bathtubs. According to them, these "people" did not merit assistance, and the Roosevelt Administration's programs to assist them were simply wasting taxpayers' money. They considered "that man in the White House" an awful traitor to his class, and thought he should be banished from political life. If there was any white person they hated more than FDR, it was his wife, Eleanor. They frowned on her support for the right of the working classes to organize those horrible labor unions. They were appalled that she had dared to invite blacks to the White House and thought that a First Lady had no business engaging in such radical activities.

Rather she should spend her time in proper activities for a wife and mother. My arguments in support of the Roosevelts (that they deserved our help in their work against segregation and poverty) fell on deaf ears. Instead of listening to my arguments, they attacked me as a radical Yale student who was undoubtedly secretly a communist. <u>Though distressing, these encounters with people of such unabashed prejudice did open my eyes to the fact that blind hatred can be found among people of any class, any religion, from any region of the country, and that it's not easy to combat.</u>

In the spring of 1942, when my time at Yale was nearing an end and it was certain that I would graduate, I sought ordination as a Baptist minister. Mary Frances and I wanted to return South, but thought that I'd have a better chance of receiving the approval of an ordination council in the North than in the South. Once ordained in the Baptist church, a minister could then serve anywhere. Dr. Gaines, my minister in Waterbury, helped me out a lot here, arranging for my examination by the ordaining council of the New Haven Baptist Association. (My theology professor, D.C. Macintosh was a member of the council.) When I did receive the council's approval, Dr. Gaines planned and conducted the ordination service, held on a Sunday evening in the First Baptist Church of Waterbury. I was grateful to him for his help and for the ecumenical tone of the service. Professor H. Richard Niebuhr, a minister in the Evangelical and Reformed Church, graciously accepted my invitation and preached the ordination sermon. Among the others who participated in the service and the laying on of hands were the president of the Waterbury Council of Churches (an Episcopal minister), and a black minister whose church held membership in the council. Needless to say, few church services have been as personally meaningful to me as that one. I suspect that few Baptist ordination services have ever been so ecumenical either. Certainly nothing of the sort would have taken place in a Southern Baptist Church. My one regret was that my father was unable to attend.

As the spring term was drawing to a close, Mary Frances and I became concerned about my securing a pastorate. One of the common quips among divinity students was that after ordination and finishing school, a Yale Divinity graduate had to get married and have three churches (instead of kids---not a good joke, but one I heard a lot). At the time, having been away from home for three years and having few contacts in the Southern

Baptist Denomination (other than my father), I had no prospects for a church in my own beloved South, to which I wanted to return.

I don't remember how it came to pass that we were invited to visit a small Georgia church just south of Augusta, but we were. Since there was no hotel, we stayed in the home of a deacon. At dinner we met "Miss" Lucy, a woman of mature years who soon made it abundantly clear that she was a pharisaical legalist, a strict fundamentalist, and the person who dominated the congregation. She informed us that, among other things, she (and thus, the church) was opposed to women wearing short sleeve dresses, boys and girls sharing the same swimming pool, and anyone going to the movies. But that wasn't all. She often presided at the church's Sunday morning service and was responsible for its format. Later, Mary Frances and I agreed that we could never lead a church dominated by one person, especially one domineering person with such a long list of "don'ts." Our host looked on Miss Lucy as a saint, and, on Sunday night, as we were leaving, remarked that he "…could not understand how God could permit her to suffer the tragedy of her daughter's running away from home." It made perfect sense to us. The poor girl probably reached the end of her rope under the thumb of the authoritative fundamentalism and the legalism of her mother. We were quite certain that we could not either.

Still without prospects, one day I voiced my concern over my future to a fellow student from the South. Even though he was a Methodist, he knew of a Baptist church which was without a minister in his former hometown of Andrews, South Carolina. The chairman of the board of deacons at the church was a friend of his, and he wrote him on my behalf. Later, we were invited to visit, and was offered and accepted the position of minister in this church, my first pastorate.

Sandra Louise Ayers

CHAPTER THREE

MINISTER AND STUDENT DIRECTOR IN SOUTH CAROLINA 1942-1949

"It was a little surprising that a Southern Baptist church would employ a Yale Divinity School graduate as its minister."

In the summer of 1942 Mary Frances and I moved to Andrews, South Carolina. Life in this small, predominantly rural, community of less than two thousand people was considerably different from life in New Haven and Waterbury, Connecticut. Although the church and the parsonage were only about a block off of Main Street, the church's street was not paved. This led to some discomfort caused by the dust and the mud. The structure of the actual church was a relatively new brick building, but it only contained the sanctuary. There was no kitchen. There was no recreation hall. There weren't even rooms for educational work in the building. Sunday School classes and Sunday evening youth meetings were held in a couple of nearby old frame buildings (one was the original small sanctuary), but they, too, had no kitchens or recreational facilities.

The parsonage was a six-room frame house with front and back porches, but no "modern" conveniences, like central heating or air conditioning, an electric cook stove or an electric hot water heater. Since the house was not insulated, not weather stripped, and not underpinned, it was very hot in the summer and very cold in the winter. In the winter we could only heat a couple of individual rooms with wood- or coal-burning space heaters. The cook stove was coal burning, and we had to make a fire in it not only to cook our meals, but also to heat the water tank to have hot water for bathing. So it was that we had fewer conveniences than we had previously enjoyed and that most of the leading members of the congregation possessed, but we were young and able to cope with these difficulties.

It was a little surprising that a Southern Baptist church would employ a Yale Divinity School graduate as its minister, rather than someone from one of the Southern Baptist seminaries. In the middle of the 19th century, Baptists in the South had withdrawn from the American Baptists over the issue of slavery and formed the Southern Baptist Convention. Since that time, Southern Baptist churches generally tended to be more theologically and socially conservative than American (Northern) Baptists. However, the fact that my father was a Southern Baptist minister probably had some influence on the church's decision. More important than that was the fact that the previous minister, who was technically in retirement during his time in Andrews, was rather theologically liberal for a Southern Baptist minister. Having my degree from a Northern and nondenominational school like Yale, and my theological "liberalism," especially with respect to ecumenism, was not, then, a problem for the majority of the congregation.

After some months of adjusting to the task of preparing two sermons each week, of working with the board of deacons and other church officials, and of meeting the congregants in their homes, I felt that the congregation would be willing to take two small steps toward ecumenicalism. A widely accepted belief among Southern Baptists was that only "true believers" of the Baptist persuasion should partake of the Lord's Supper, and thus they practiced "closed communion," which excluded any visitors from other Christian churches. Also, they believed that the only genuine sign of a person's regeneration was "baptism by immersion" (the form of baptism described in the New Testament), and so they required that new members or converts be rebaptized in their tradition. The issue was the abandonment of these practices, the acceptance of open communion, and the possibility of allowing other non-Baptists to join them without being rebaptized.

I sought to lay the groundwork for such a progressive move through sermons and teaching classes, emphasizing church history. The major principle of the historical Baptist movement, beginning as early as the 16th century with the Anabaptists or Anti-pedobaptists, was that the congregation of the church should be made up of spiritually regenerated people. It wasn't the FORM of baptism that concerned the early Baptists, but the act itself. Many of them practiced pouring rather than immersion.

Many Southern Baptists were also against the practice of infant baptism. Under the (then) prevailing circumstances, infant baptism was bound up with the idea of a State Church with its members having been baptized as infants and many of whom were total strangers to a vital Christian experience. The question at hand was whether or not the infantally-baptized were repentant. Do babies have anything to repent for?

The early Anabaptist insistence about only baptizing the believers and the restriction of church membership to the equally-faithful may be understood as a protective principle intended to protect the ideal of a spiritual church. Given our vastly different circumstances today (today then---the 1940s), I argued that we no longer needed those protective principles. They only served to separate us.

The fact was that, despite what some people thought, there was no State Church where everyone was baptized as infants. Our Baptist forebears in America (such as Roger Williams, who went to Rhode Island seeking religious freedom) played a large role in the establishment of the separation of church and state and of religious freedom. Today, church membership is voluntary. Many Christians, especially Protestants, do not even regard baptism as essential to salvation. Salvation is now generally thought to be exclusively dependent on the inner disposition of the believer with grateful acceptance of God's love.

Generally those churches that practice infant baptism regard that rite as a symbol of the seal of God's love applied to the infant and of the parents' commitment to nurture the child in the Christian faith such that he or she will come to that inner disposition of love for God and other people. It is only after the child reaches the age of accountability and attends confirmation classes (instruction in the Christian faith) that he or she becomes a full-fledged member of the church. Therefore, to invite all Christians to participate in the communion service and to partake of the elements and to accept Christians from other denominations for membership without rebaptism do not endanger the fundamental Baptist principle of a spiritually regenerated church body. <u>Indeed, the one rightly indispensable condition of membership in a Christian church is that a person sincerely seeks to be Christian in faith, experience and purpose</u>. Recognizing this, British Baptists and American Baptists of the Northern Convention long ago abandoned closed communion and received, by letter, Christians of other denominations into their church membership.

There were some of the more influential members of the church who in previous years had been embarrassed by the practice of closed communion, of having visiting friends or relatives of other denominations excluded from the communion service, and of requiring rebaptism of those from other denominations who wished to join our church. Therefore, they were receptive to the conclusions of my historical analysis. The board of deacons unanimously approved a resolution recommending that the entire congregation vote to abandon those two practices. The resolution was presented to the congregation in its regular business meeting. In the discussion which preceded the vote, one or two of the more conservative members proclaimed that in a publication of the Southern Baptist Sunday School Board it had been declared that the official position of the Southern Baptist Convention required the observance of these two odious practices. Supporters of the deacons' resolution pointed out that historically Baptists have insisted on freedom from externally binding creeds, freedom of scriptural interpretation, and independence of the local church. Given the Baptist principle of congregational autonomy, the local church was not compelled to accept everything which came from some denominational agency. In spite of rejecting some things, we would still send part of the church's income to the denominational agencies and were still committed to <u>basic</u> Baptist principles, such as a spiritual church, religious freedom, and the idea of separation of church and state. The deacons' resolution passed easily, and was entered in the minutes as the official position of the Andrews Baptist Church.

While some progress was made with respect to theological and ecclesiastical issues, I encountered an adamant resistance to any suggestions concerning the changing of attitudes and practices with respect to social issues, such as race relations and the plight of sharecroppers. One of our church members, a leading merchant in town, rented to a group of shacks on one of the town's back alleys to black families. These shacks had no glass windows, no screens, no indoor plumbing of any sort, and had only one collective water faucet for the entire neighborhood to share. Some people called them "shotgun shacks." This merchant was not a Simon Legree, but was courteous and friendly in his personal relationships. He made generous contributions to the church and helped us secure a much-needed heater for the parsonage. When I discovered that he owned the shacks and asked if he did not think he had a Christian duty to improve them, especially with regard to sanitation, even if it meant smaller profits for him, <u>his response was that his ownership of the shacks was a matter of business and had nothing to do with his Christian faith</u>. He could not understand why I would raise such a question, for he thought my job as a minister was to save souls, not to meddle in economic or political matters. The same attitude was prevalent among large farm owners of the congregation (the merchant also owned a farm, along with a few other congregants) who had sharecroppers on their land. <u>I encountered this idea of a separation of church and life all too often</u>.

Andrews was located on the coastal plain of South Carolina, and its culture and economy were mainly dominated by large farming interests. With the exception of some who had jobs in a paper mill about twenty miles away, most people worked the farms, in farm-related businesses, or in mercantile establishments. The town's "establishment," political and social, was made up of farm owners, merchants, a few professionals. Such an environment was new to me. While at Yale I had learned of and joined the Fellowship of Southern Churchmen, a small group of liberal ministers and laity concerned with the major social issues in the South. Through its literature and my courses in Social Ethics I had read about the plight of sharecroppers, but until Andrews I had no first-hand experience with the situation. But I learned.

During the time we were in Andrews I saw the sharecropping life up close. I visited some of our members who were owners, still living in the "home places" on their farms, and sometimes encountered their tenants, occasionally visiting them in their shacks, especially when there was an illness in the family (that's when people call their preachers). To this day, I remember visiting a tenant family on a cold winter day and sitting huddled around a smoking fireplace. The fire was small. They needed to conserve their meager wood supply. In spite of the small fire and the cold, a window near the fireplace was kept open, so that when they needed more wood they could just reach out the window. Unsurprisingly, some of them had respiratory problems.

My experience of rural life in the vicinity of Andrews was augmented by virtue of the fact that, for a period of time, I served as minister of a second church, a small country church which held services on Sunday afternoons. The board of deacons of the Andrews church approved of my taking on the additional responsibility, in spite of my own slight misgivings about it. I suspected that they felt the small payment I would receive from the second church would relieve them of any obligation to raise my salary, which was the princely sum of $1800 per year (heavenly reward versus earthly riches and all that). Had it not been for my brother, James, I would not have been able to afford an automobile, an absolute necessity in such a rural place. At any rate, I served this country church for about a year. Then, much to my surprise, I learned that the church had a policy they named a "yearly call." One Sunday afternoon an itinerant type of "preacher" appeared, demanding to be heard (apparently he knew about the "yearly call" policy). The congregation voted to hear him. Since I felt the congregation had not dealt fairly with me by not telling me about this when they had asked me to serve, and since the work was often frustrating, took time away from my work at Andrews, and was a huge energy drain, I resigned, an action which seemed to make little difference to the church leadership.

From a few of my supporters I learned that the dissatisfaction with me on the parts of several influential members of this little country church had been growing and was due to several factors. First, I had attempted to influence some of the young people by teaching them myself in a large class. Sometimes the adults would listen in (there was only one church sanctuary and it was small). They didn't like what they heard, though it was mainly Bible study and not very radical. Second, they thought my sermons were not "full of the Spirit," but too intellectual and too radical. Third, they disapproved of the attention I'd been paying the sharecropper families, visiting them and inviting them to attend church. They thought the sharecroppers would feel out-of-place in the church, which they did, feeling as if their clothes weren't nice enough for The Lord's House. In spite of my assurances that clothes didn't matter, they felt embarrassed to wear their country rags to church and so they didn't attend. Of course, this was all symbolic of a larger issue, the rigid class structure in this rural community that existed long before I got there.

Like the cotton mill workers in the Piedmont of my youth, the sharecroppers were on the lowest rung of the class structure in the predominantly agricultural region, but their living conditions and educational opportunities were even worse than those of the mill workers. Their shacks were smaller and without window glass, and their children were kept out of school (which were, themselves, generally poor in quality) for extended periods of time in order to assist their parents with the work in the fields. Just as the mill workers bought on credit from the company store, so the sharecroppers bought on credit from the crossroads store, which was usually owned by the owner of the very land on which they toiled without possibility of advancement. During the months leading up to the harvest they incurred debts at these stores that they were unable to pay off when the crops were harvested. It's the same cycle. And, when the crops were poor because of unfavorable weather conditions, it was virtually impossible for them to pay off their debts. Unlike mill workers, who at least could quit their jobs and move elsewhere, many sharecroppers were enslaved, as bound to the land as medieval serfs, because of their debts to the land owners. Often the owners would threaten them with arrest (law enforcement, then and now, did and does the bidding of the ownership class) if they attempted to leave, and would give them even larger amounts of crops to harvest. In many ways, the plight of the sharecropper was similar to that of blacks during the days of slavery.

The practice of sharecropping was so deeply embedded in the structure of Southern agriculture that it seemed impervious to change. My small and hesitant efforts to bring some change in attitude were rather fruitless. In one of my sermons in the Andrews church I referred to sharecropping as a social evil. I later learned from the Methodist minister in town that some of the farm-owners in my congregation had gone to him to complain about the sermon and seeking assurance from a preacher, any preacher, that sharecropping was not a sin. I didn't ask the minister how he'd responded to them, but in any case, the landowners of the town had me in their sights and were actively mounting a campaign against me.

The strange thing is that many of the church leaders actually agreed with my theological perspective. That and the fact that the area youth had begun to attend church were probably the only things that kept the torches and pitchforks at bay. The kids liked me because I practiced football with them. For real. I used to put on pads, scrimmage with them, and engage them in active religion. Football and Christianity are the peas and carrots of the rural American South. I was even able to organize a group of townsmen (former football players themselves) for a charity benefit game where they played against the current high school football team on one of their open dates. It was rather amusing watching the former football players, whose weight had increased considerably since their playing days, attempting to squeeze into their old high school uniforms. We insisted, of course, that the coach play on our team. We lost, but it was a decent game and a lot of fun. Practically the whole town turned out for the event, and we made a considerable amount of money. Interestingly, some of the high school players began showing up for our Sunday morning services.

In a valiant, but doomed, attempt to change the sharecropping system, some members of the Fellowship of Southern Churchmen engaged in courageous actions which brought upon them reprisals of one sort or another. In one case in another state, a few members sought to organize the farm workers, including sharecroppers, into a union. The leader of this group was tarred and feathered and transported to the state line. The media barely noticed. It may be that such brave works which brought such drastic persecution had some influence for change in the long run, but they had little immediate effect and were not the principle causes for the demise of the system.

The real reasons that sharecropping died out were many. The fact that World War II brought higher prices for farm products and many sharecroppers were able to pay off their debts and leave the farm helped. Also, many of their sons of draft age fought in the war, and the old World War I refrain of, "How are you going to keep them down on the farm when they have seen gay Paree?" was certainly applicable. With the help of the G.I. Bill, after the war some were able to secure college degrees which prepared them for good, higher-paying jobs. Finally, the growth of technology and mechanization in agriculture made certain types of manual labor obsolete, and so reduced the need for the manpower provided by the sharecropping system. <u>While the evils associated with sharecropping have largely disappeared, it seems they have been replaced with another major social problem in agriculture, namely, the plight of migrant workers.</u>

As indicated above, our years in Andrews were WWII years. I had received deferment from military service because of my status as an ordained minister, but I was neither a pacifist nor a warmonger. My position was similar to Reinhold Neibuhr's. The war was not some holy crusade, but as all wars, it was a social evil. Yet it was a lesser evil than that of permitting Hitler's aggression, slaughter of millions of non-combatants (especially in the concentration camps), and the threat of a completely-Nazi Europe, if not an entire world. For this reason, I supported the war effort in ways that were available to me, but at the same time sought to point out to members of our congregation in conversations and sermons that the stereotyped picture presented in the hysterical propaganda of the time was greatly exaggerated and not true of the majority of the German and Japanese people.

I mentioned above the itinerant and self-designated preacher who had shown up one Sunday at the country church. Another such preacher, who worked for the railroad, joined the Andrews church. He held extreme apocalyptic views, insisting that the gasoline rationing cards of the war years were the "Mark of the Beast" of Revelation and that the end of the world was near. He sought to become the teacher of the men's Bible class, and a few favored him because "he was a good talker." However, the majority felt that his views were too extreme and, with my urging, refused to accept him as their teacher, insisting that the teacher they had already (a thoughtful lay person) be kept in that position.

One of my memorable experiences in Andrews was that of preaching, at the invitation of the minister, in the local Black church. I was impressed by the vitality and spirit of the congregation and the hospitality and goodwill extended to me. Confronted by this, I felt guilty and was distressed by the fact that I enjoyed a privileged life denied to them and that my congregation would not permit me to reciprocate their invitation. I found that preaching to this congregation was one of the most difficult things I had ever done. The question that plagued me was how could I, in such a situation, avoid any taint of unwitting hypocrisy. I could not presume upon my status as a Yale graduate and ordained minister to claim to be in possession of some **special** divine information service as to **precisely** what God thought and willed for them in their life situations, with which I had little experience. On the one hand, I did not feel that it was appropriate for **me** to preach about loving neighbors (including white neighbors) in the context of a racist and segregated society. On the other hand, it would have been irresponsible for me in a sermon to inspire them to actively or even passively engage in an assault on segregation with all the reprisals, the persecution, and the suffering this would bring upon them.

As I recall, in my sermon I sought to deal with the problem of personal suffering (illness and the death of loved ones) in light of the love of God. If God is Love, as the New Testament claims, then it is a mistaken notion that God is directly responsible for even a single instance of suffering. Whatever the causes of suffering may be (our acts, the acts of other people, or chance events), God is the loving fellow sufferer who understands and seeks to provide us, if we are willing, with the strength to meet anything which might happen to us. They were rightfully proud of their young men fighting in the war, but if by chance, contrary to our hopes, some of them died, they could depend on the love of God to sustain them in their sorrow. They seemed to appreciate the sermon, but most of all the fact that I, a white minister, would even participate in their service.

After two years in Andrews, Mary Frances and I had our first child, Sandra Louise. There was no hospital in Andrews and we had planned to have the delivery in a hospital some twenty miles away. However, when Mary Frances went into labor, our local doctor, who had been summoned in the middle of the night, informed us that the birth was about to take place and there wasn't time to get to the hospital. We had not made any plans for such an eventuality and were without help of any kind when the doctor and his nurse left. Sandra thrived somewhat better than her mother who, on doctor's orders, remained in bed for two weeks, so long that most of her strength was depleted, and it would be several months before she felt her old self again.

In the spring of 1945 (we had been in Andrews almost four years) I received a personal letter from the Executive Director of the General Board of the South Carolina Baptist Convention. The General Board (the members of which are elected by and from the convention), through its agencies, carries out the policies decided upon by the state convention at its yearly meetings, meets several times a year when the convention is not in session in order to settle any issues which need immediate resolution, and oversees the work of several state agencies such as the Department of Missions, Student Work, etc. The Executive Director held a top-salaried position and was responsible to the Board for the work of the several departments. Needless to say, I was a bit surprised, puzzled, and somewhat apprehensive at receiving a letter from such an important person in the South Carolina Baptist hierarchy, especially since he indicated a desire to visit us. I suspected, naturally, that he wished to investigate my soundness as to "Southern Baptist Doctrine." In spite of my apprehension, I invited him to visit with us over a weekend and to preach at our Sunday morning service.

It turned out that his visit had nothing to do with my theology or work in Andrews. Much to my delighted surprise, in the course of our private conversations, he inquired as to whether or not I would be interested in the position of Director of the Department of Baptist Student Work in South Carolina. I was puzzled as to why he would approach me, a Yale Divinity School graduate, and later was to learn that the minister of the First Baptist Church in Columbia (across the street from the state headquarters building), who was an old friend of my father's, had suggested that I might be a prospect to replace the retiring state director of the Baptist Student Union.

I was interested in the position because I felt that it would be possible to wield a greater influence with young people in terms of changing attitudes concerning Christian and social ethics that it was with the socially-conservative people of Andrews. Then, too, the very fact that I had not attended a Southern Baptist seminary, but rather had a degree from Yale, would make a statement to the Baptist students of the state.

The position was offered. I accepted, and in the late summer of 1945 we moved to Columbia. At this time housing in the city was in short supply. We were able to find only a rather small upstairs apartment in a home in an older section of the city. Though a bit cramped for space, we were fairly comfortable, except during the long periods of summer when the heat in Columbia soars, and everyone suffers from heat rash, especially babies.

In the weeks before the colleges and universities in the state opened, I sought to familiarize myself with the duties of the Director of the Baptist Student Union in South Carolina and the status of the local units on the campuses in the state. My duties included visiting the campuses, helping to organize local units where there were none, encouraging and strengthening those units without local directors, and counseling with the few local directors at the larger colleges. In addition, there was the planning for two major state-wide events during the year, namely the spring retreat (primarily a planning session for the local and state student officers) and the fall convention, open to any and all South Carolina Baptists. These conventions had gotten popular with students, with as many as a thousand students attending the weekend sessions.

I was also responsible for the summer so-called Youth Revivals. As you can imagine, I had some misgivings about that. Students volunteered for this program, and each was assigned to one of the churches which had made a request for a revival. These students had to attend a weeklong training session, which I thought wholly inadequate preparation for the work they were going to have to do at the revivals. Fortunately, to the best of my knowledge, these kids did little or no harm. In most cases they were merely counselors for the church's youth, and did not preach, except at one or two services. As I recall, working out the details of this program was difficult and frustrating, especially for a liberal like me.

After I'd been in this position for about a year, I was once again surprised when the General Secretary called me into his office and informed me that <u>a committee from the Greenville Baptist Ministerial Society was going to assemble in his office the next Monday to question me about the soundness of my faith</u>. It was a Dr. Gezork witch hunt/Inquisition all over again. I was starting to see a pattern. In truth, it was just history repeating itself once again. As I was to learn later, they formed this committee in order to appease one of its fundamentalist members who had accused me of holding heretical views. I had never even met the man, and yet that didn't stop him of calling me a heretic.

In the hearing/Inquisition, where my accuser (fairly or unfairly) also sat in judgment of me, it became clear that this fundamentalist's charges against me were based on a letter he had received from a young woman sent by his local church (not the Southern Baptist Mission Board) to Brazil as a missionary. Copies of the state Baptist newsletter had been sent to her, and in one she read of my appointment to my new job as state Director of the Baptist Student Union. She wrote to my accuser, stating that, while at Furman, she had overheard me defending Dr. Gezork and "<u>ridiculing the blood</u>." In response, I told the committee that yes, I had proudly defended Dr. Gezork, but I was but one of many, and I remembered neither the young lady nor having "ridiculed the blood." Only if some magical property was claimed for this substance (as in the Catholic view of sacramental wine becoming the blood of Christ), I might as a college student have ridiculed this view (making fun of Catholics was a popular Southern Baptists pastime then). <u>If this expression is simply a symbolic way of referring to Christ's sacrifice on the cross, I most certainly did not ridicule that, for it is an essential pillar of the Christian faith</u>. Furthermore, I was fully committed to those historical

Baptist principles of a spiritually-regenerate church body, the individual's freedom to interpret Scripture for himself, under the guidance of the Holy Spirit, and the independence of religion and separation of church and state.

I concluded my defense by saying that it didn't seem quite fair to hold one responsible now for what he may have said as a student, almost ten years previously. Had this committee never met a teenager? Young people sometimes make extreme statements to shock opponents, not necessarily because they genuinely hold this or that position. The fact that the fundamentalist minister had even initiated this "heresy trial" on the basis of what I was supposedly overheard saying a decade earlier appeared to have been news to the other committee members, and most of them were rightfully embarrassed when the truth came out. I was (and still am) amazed that seemingly intelligent people would launch a heresy hunt without at least first ascertaining the facts, and I said as much. I've never been one to keep my mouth shut. In times like those, that can be a blessing. Also, I asked why no one had come to me personally and privately to ask me about my beliefs, but rather had chosen to hurl accusations at me in a public forum on the basis of unsubstantiated claims. The fundamentalist minister was infuriated. <u>He vociferously proclaimed that they (the committee) were there to question me, and not the other way around</u>. He kept repeating that he was not satisfied by my answers, that I was simply covering up my heretical beliefs, and that I was attempting to lead our Baptist youth into heretical "modernism."

Although they did not take a formal vote, most of the committee members indicated, by their statements, that they were satisfied that I had sound Baptist principles, even though the fundamentalist minister leveled a charge of "cover up" against them and the General Secretary. At any rate, I was not charged with heresy. Naively, I thought they would report their finding to the Greenville Baptist Ministers Association, but years later I learned they hadn't. Remember this. It later added to another problem I'll get to after a while.

Another heresy trial! This time I was the accused heretic. Of course, our Lord was called heretic, and worse, by the Philistines of His day, too (not that I'm comparing myself, but the irony is worth noting).

One of the most vivid memories I have of the hearing was a statement made by one of the committee members as he was leaving the meeting. He was the minister of one of the largest churches in an industrial village in Greenville, and he said to me, "I am satisfied now, but I'm going to keep my eye on you." Several months later, a newborn baby was found on the steps of his parsonage, and it turned out that it was his child by a young female friend of his daughter. Eventually, he had to leave the church, even though, according to reports, some of his members wanted to forgive him and keep him on. Christianity is all about forgiveness, after all. For some of his fundamentalist friends, adultery seemed less immoral than holding unorthodox beliefs. Even later, I read a newspaper account of his being arrested for some minor crime.

I managed to survive this fundamentalist assault and continued to work with Baptist students. Most of the local and state officers were intelligent young people, genuinely concerned about Christian life and alleviating the suffering and injustice in the world. They were eager to gain a more profound and vital understanding of the Christian faith. The student officers at the state level, in consultation with me and some other adult advisors, sought to plan programs for the state conventions which were not limited to the usual evangelistic and individualistic nature of most of these programs. Instead, they dealt with some of the more profound theological and social issues of the day. They invited not only some younger progressive and thoughtful ministers to participate, but also others who were doing significant work in other fields. Among the latter was a young man from South Carolina who was a student at Harvard and the president of the American (Northern) Baptist Students Movement, the president of the Southern Regional Council (a professor at Coker College in SC), an organization seeking to improve race relations in the South, and a young man with a degree from Union Theological Seminary who was working with the Textile Workers Union in the state.

While the majority of the students attending these state conventions found the programs interesting and challenging, there was a small, but loud, group of fundamentalist students from a small fundamentalist college who were disturbed by their newly progressive nature, and they, predictably, complained to their ministers. This was to hold some sway a few years later, when, once again, charges were brought against me.

Another duty of the state director was to encourage the Baptist students in the state to attend Student Week at Ridgecrest in the North Carolina mountains; the summer assembly grounds of the Southern Baptist Convention. The program for this week was planned by the Director and staff of the entire Baptist Student Movement of the Southern Baptist Convention. With a few exceptions, the addresses at the plenary sessions were rather conventional and traditional. The most creative talks and discussions were generally to be found in the small seminars and group sessions.

I now find it somewhat surprising that I first met the radical Christian Clarence Jordan, during a student week at Ridgecrest. Clarence was the founder of the Christian community in Georgia known as the Koinonia Farms, and the translator of the Greek New Testament into the English version called the Cotton Patch version. A graduate of the University of Georgia College of Agriculture and a Ph.D. in the Greek New Testament from the Southern Baptist Theological Seminary, Clarence was a person of unusual talents, combining scholarship with practical expertise, compassion for the poor and oppressed, humility and an extraordinary sense of humor. At Koinonia he sought to establish a Christian community which would approximate the kingdom of God on earth. There were no barriers of race and creed, and all property was held in common.

His descriptions of life at Koinonia, his vision of the Christian life, his humor, and the attractiveness of his personality made him popular with large numbers of students at Ridgecrest. They listened to his messages with keen interest and enthusiasm. In spite of this, or perhaps because of it, the adult authorities who planned the student week program, to the best of my knowledge, never again invited Clarence to participate in this program.

Many years later I had an opportunity to visit Koinonia, and to observe the community's structure, lifestyle, and successful farming operation. The families in the community were housed in separate apartments in a couple of remodeled farm houses, while the few single men had rooms in another structure which also had room for guests. I remember that I accepted Clarence's invitation to spend the night, and was rudely awakened at 4 AM by the loud clucking of the innumerable chickens in the nearby chicken house. At breakfast I proclaimed a deep sympathy for the poor, sleep-deprived chickens, not to mention the human beings, but was informed that this did not bother the chickens, who produced more eggs when awakened early. At that time the sale of eggs was one of the major sources of income for the community.

My most vivid memory from this visit was sitting in his apartment with Clarence (he was dressed in work clothes after having plowed a field earlier), discussing the historical Jesus' vision of the Kingdom of God and other New Testament issues. On this occasion, as was his custom in all discussions and speeches, he used his well-worn Greek New Testament. I also recall that Clarence mentioned several things that had been done by Koinonia to help improve the agricultural methods used by farmers in the surrounding community, and at some point in our discussion he deplored the poor housing in which many, especially blacks, were forced to live. It is not generally known, but the inspiration and beginning of the Habitat for Humanity program was at Koinonia. The first houses were built on Koinonia property, and Millard Fuller, who developed the program into a national and world-wide affair, was a member of Koinonia before he became the full-time director of the Habitat for Humanity program.

My greatest success as Director of the South Carolina Baptist Student Union, at least as far as the Director of the B.S.U. for the entire South (my boss) and the General Board of the S.C. Baptist Convention were concerned, was to purchase a rather large two-story house adjacent to the University of South Carolina to serve as the student center for the Baptist students at this university. At the formal opening of the center, a service of dedication was held in which the Southwide Director of the B.S.U. and the General Secretary of the S.C. Baptist Convention were the major participants. As I recall, I experienced some embarrassment at this service. We held it in the large library, with its attractive fireplace, and, since it was a cool day, I thought it would be pleasant to have an open fire. Unfortunately, however, the flue did not draw properly and the room soon filled with smoke. We quickly extinguished the fire and opened the doors and windows to dispel the smoke, but the smell lingered on during the service and there was some coughing in the audience.

The upstairs rooms of the house had been made into two apartments, one of which was occupied by the young woman who was Director of the B.S.U. at the University of South Carolina and the other by my family. This made it convenient to have adult supervision in the center, so it was open most of the time. The downstairs of the house was arranged in such a way (large sliding doors between many of the rooms) that made it possible to have fairly large group meetings as well as smaller ones, and even some dinner meetings. There was a rather large hallway, on one side of which was the large library with a smaller room behind it serving as an office for the local director. Off the far side of the library was a large sunroom with a ping pong table and other recreational equipment. On the other side of the hallway were the living room, the dining room, and the kitchen. Students came to the center not only for meetings and for vespers, but also to play games, talk, and study. It soon became evident that the presence of the center had helped to invigorate and expand the B.S.U. program at the university.

There was one mildly amusing incident when we were living at the center. One evening after dinner I went downstairs with the hope of engaging in a ping pong match. I noticed that the large sliding doors that separated the hallway from the living room were closed. It was our policy to keep all the sliding doors open, except when the room was being used for a group meeting. Nothing was scheduled for this particular evening, so I opened the doors and found it occupied by a young couple (a boy and a girl), sitting rather close together on the sofa. They were strangers to me, and I asked them if they were students at the university and if they were interested in joining the B.S.U. They informed me that they were students from a Bible College in the city, that they were prayer-mates, and had closed the doors in order to pray as the Bible instructed. Since I was aware of the harsh rules and strict separation of the sexes at this college, I was somewhat sympathetic with this couple, who may have been engaging in a more common type of college student religious ritual than they'd admitted. I told them they could stay as long as they wished, but that it was our policy to keep the doors open except for group meetings. Then I invited them to attend our vespers, where they would have an opportunity to engage in both public and private prayer. I wish I could report that this couple immediately joined the B.S.U., but, to the best of my knowledge, they never came to center again. Maybe the Methodists have more private rooms.

It was while we were living in the center that Mary Frances and I had our second child, Charles Jerry, on April 16, 1948. Unlike Sandra, he was delivered in a Columbia hospital instead of at home. Our major problem when we took him home from the hospital was eliminating a skin rash, which had developed as a result of the use of a particular baby oil prescribed by the pediatrician. This required several visits to a dermatologist, but soon little Charles Jerry was well and thriving. In spite of some minor problems (such as the heat of the Columbia summers), for the most part our life in the student center was enjoyable, and our relationship with the students invigorating and often inspiring.

The relative tranquility (after my earlier inquisition) of our life and work in South Carolina was brought to an abrupt halt in the 1948-1949 academic year. At one of the meetings of The General Board of the S.C. Baptist Convention, when the state workers were reappointed for another year, a member of the Board who was a minister in Aiken, S.C. and had been a chaplain in World War II, objected when my name came up for consideration. He claimed that I was a modernist and a pacifist, and thus not fit to work with young people. Unfortunately, a previously scheduled speaking engagement at a college in a distant city made it impossible for me to attend this meeting, and so I was not there to defend myself. Later I heard that someone asked him what evidence he had for such charges. He withdrew the modernist charge, but claimed that one of his congregation's college students had heard me say at a meeting at his college that war was evil and anyone who died in battle went straight to hell. This, of course, was a gross misinterpretation of my position, which had been, as stated earlier, that while war IS evil, it is sometimes (as in WWII) a lesser evil. I most certainly did not believe, nor had I ever said, that anyone who participated in a war and died in battle went straight to hell. Such a statement is obviously absurd. I was not a pacifist, but even if I had been, that should not have been sufficient grounds for not reappointing me.

Later I learned that this minister suffered from very serious mental and emotional problems and eventually became a patient in the state mental hospital. One of my friends, a local B.S.U. Director, once jokingly remarked that even if he knew for a fact that I was a blatant agnostic or had done some terrible deed, he "would not touch me with a ten-foot pole," for just look at what happened to the two ministers who had brought charges against me. One was in prison and the other in a mental hospital.

Since I worked with students and had little contact with most of the Baptist ministers in the state, very few members of the General Board had first-hand knowledge of my outlook and beliefs. One of two were from college towns and knew me, but were not strong in their support of me. In spite of the absurdity of the charges, the members of the General Board voted approval of a motion that stated that, while I could continue to work and be paid, I should not be formally reappointed, for that would make the Board liable to pay my salary for a full year even though they had decided to terminate my employment. The motion also instructed the General Secretary to appoint a small committee of five members of the Board (designated as the student affairs committee) to investigate and to report its findings at the next Board meeting.

The "student affairs committee" held a meeting at which they heard from several sources, but they never once requested that I appear before them. I later learned that the committee had listened to some fundamentalist ministerial students who complained that our state programs were not evangelistic enough. It was claimed that as a member of the interracial Fellowship of Southern Churchmen (something I never sought to hide and was proud of), having taken my family to the interracial summer retreats of this group, I held radical left-wing social views which were having some influence on students by means of state programs and my work in religious emphasis weeks.

While it was never mentioned specifically in any of the charges leveled against me, my support of integration, of the 1948 Truman-era Democratic Party's civil rights platform plank "to eradicate all racial, religious, and economic discrimination," undoubtedly further antagonized many of those who opposed me on theological grounds. The social milieu of South Carolina was permeated by conservatism, and this conservatism had been augmented by its governor, Strom Thurmond. At the time, Thurmond was a Democrat, but in reaction to the civil rights plank took the South Carolina delegation out of the 1948 Democratic Convention. He formed the so-called "Dixiecrat Party," ran for president, and carried the four states of Alabama, Louisiana, Mississippi, and South Carolina. This was probably the presage of a Republican surge in the South. Thurmond later joined the Republican Party, and was elected the U.S. Senator from South Carolina.

Early in his tenure as South Carolina governor, a popular journal, which was publishing a series of articles on religion by elected officials, asked Thurmond to write an article. At the request of his office (an assistant had heard me make a speech on religion), I had "ghost-written" a rough draft of the governor's article, and even received a note of thanks from Thurmond. When he withdrew from the Democratic Party and ran for president, I, along with my friend Maxie Collins (the founder of a rehabilitation center for alcoholics) and other loyal Democrats opposed him, seeking to keep South Carolina in the Democratic fold. We lost in South Carolina, but the Democrats won the national election (just barely, this was the "Dewey Defeats Truman" election). All of my adult life I have been registered as a Democrat, and voted for the Party's candidate for president. Most of the time I have voted for the Democratic candidates for local and state offices, believing that probably the best chances for improving the lot of those subjected to poverty and discrimination would come from the Democrats at the national, state, and local levels.

In addition to the charge that the state B.S.U. programs were not evangelistic enough, one member of the hearing committee, a minister in Greenville, claimed that the earlier committee from the Greenville Ministerial Association had never made a report to this body exonerating me of my previous charges. Also, someone informed the committee that during the previous summer I had studied at Union Theological Seminary in New York. The General Secretary had approved a two-week extension of my regular four-week vacation in order that I might be able to attend the six-week summer session at Union. The committee came to the conclusion that by leaving the state for this period of time I had failed to give proper direction to the summer youth revival program. Actually, I had made all the plans and arranged the schedule before leaving on July 1. Since my assistant and I took our vacations at different times, we had planned for her to be in the office while I was away, in case any circumstances arose which needed the attention of our office. I was never able to present this or any other defense before the committee.

It became obvious that, despite the logical absurdity (a non-sequitur) or falsity of the charges against me, the committee had no inclination to defend me or my record. At the conclusion of their deliberations, they sent the chairman to inform me that their recommendation to the Board was that I officially be reappointed, but that I be advised to resign as soon as was feasible. If at all possible, the resignation should be submitted before the next Baptist state convention, for there were indications that some delegates would make my reappointment an issue on the floor of the convention, and the resulting publicity would hurt my career. It seemed to me that this decision of the committee was most certainly disingenuous, a spurious exoneration of me to salve their own consciences, while in fact they were firing me and putting my family at financial risk in order to protect their own careers in the political realm of South Carolina Baptists.

The late winter and early spring of 1949 was a period of considerable anxiety for me and for my family. Much of my time was occupied with searching for a job. The prospects for a pastorate in South Carolina were, of course, minimal. Two "liberal" churches which had, two years earlier contacted me about openings had already filled them. The previous summer, while I was at Union Seminary, B. David Napier, the Chaplain and Professor of Religion at the University of Georgia, had called me to inquire if I would be interested in the position of Assistant Chaplain at UGA. I had known "Davie" at Yale Divinity School, where he had been a Ph.D. candidate while I was working for my B.D. degree. I was honored that he would think of me, but at the time thought I should carry on with my important work in South Carolina, despite the fundamentalist attacks.

A scant ten months later I greatly regretted that decision. I called Davie to ask if the position was still open. It was not. The new Assistant Chaplain was a young woman/seminary graduate, Anne Queen. However, Davie told me that he had just accepted a professorship in Old Testament at Yale Divinity School, set to begin next fall, and asked if I would be interested in his position (Chaplain and Assistant Professor of Religion at UGA). My response was a strong affirmative. Was that ever a relief. During the spring, Mary Frances and I made several trips to the university for interviews with administrators, faculty, and students.

The position was offered. We accepted, and moved to Athens, Georgia in the fall of 1949.

Jeremy Ayers

CHAPTER FOUR

THE UNIVERSITY OF GEORGIA, THE EARLY YEARS: CHAPLAIN AND ASSISTANT PROFESSOR OF RELIGION, 1949-1960

"One wonders what has happened to the time-honored tradition of universities as protected communities where men and women experiment with ideas."

Any move from one city to another, from one job to another, is bound to cause problems. This was certainly the case with me when we moved to Athens. Not only did we have to secure adequate housing for a family of four, but I also had to transition to a very different type of job than the one I had held in South Carolina.

After much searching we finally managed to rent a rather small Knox house. In addition to the living room, kitchen and bath, it had two tiny bedrooms, which were barely adequate for the four of us. The landlord was not the most pleasant person in the world (and I'm being kind here), and was very reluctant to order needed repairs whenever the central floor furnace failed to function properly or the water heater stopped working.

My position at UGA involved not only responsibility for the extra-curricular religious programs on the campus, but also teaching one course per quarter. While I had worked with students in South Carolina and participated in religious programs on several campuses, I had no teaching experience. Furthermore, it had been several years since I had studied at Yale, and, except for the 1948 Summer Session at Union Seminary, I had no time in South Carolina for scholarly pursuits. Having to teach courses on World Religions and the Old and New Testaments meant that I had to spend hours studying old class notes and texts (fortunately I had kept them) in order to keep even a step ahead of the students in the class. This is what teachers do, even though few of us admit it until years later when we're writing our memoirs. Added to this difficulty was the fact that, during the first quarter at UGA I contracted a serious case of pneumonia, which put me in the hospital and away from classes for several days. My strength was slow to return, and I had to struggle just to keep up with my work. It was not an auspicious start, but even at a young age, I was used to that.

What I had inherited at UGA was a so-called Department of Religion of which I was both the head AND the only faculty member. I was in charge…of myself. Our "department" (if you can call it that) had to teach one class per quarter. Since all the courses were electives which could not be used to fulfill any kind of requirement except for hours needed for graduation or for the major in religion, enrollment was very small. Thus I made application through the dean to the executive committee of the Arts and Sciences College to add World Religions to the six social science courses offered (students had to take three). At that time, in the early 1950s, the post-war G.I. Bill students were finishing college and enrollment was decreasing. While some of the social science department heads objected to my proposal on the spurious grounds of separation of church and state (though, I've got to say that the scholarly study of and teaching about religion is an academic discipline and NOT a matter of proselytizing---it was a state university, not a fundamentalist Bible "college"), one of them was actually honest enough to admit the truth. It was about money. He told me in confidence that the "pie was split too thin already and the list should be decreased instead of augmented."

Another major difficulty encountered in those early years with respect to enrollment and the development of the Religion Department into a real department was the fact that, prior to my arrival, the Disciples of Christ had established an institution adjacent to campus known as the Christian College. In many ways this was our religious education competition. They were <u>right there next to us</u>. Even though it was called a "college" and had a "dean," it was not a degree-granting institution, but was in reality a sort of Bible chair, established for the express purpose of teaching religion at the University of Georgia. The faculty of the Arts and Sciences College had voted disapproval of this type of relationship, but the top administrators had not discouraged the Disciples from investing in buildings and staff. With this an accomplished fact, after formulating some rather stringent requirements with respect to teacher and course qualifications, the administration approved several courses not offered by the Department of Religion from which university students could elect to take three (fifteen hours). While this arrangement made it easier for the few students who needed it to secure a major in religion, there was considerable competition for those students who elected to take only one religion course.

The relationship with the Christian College endured for many years in spite of the dubious nature of such a bond and the expansion of the University's own program in religion. Eventually it was terminated, for the problems endemic to all such arrangements finally became obvious. In spite of the stringent requirements with respect to teachers and courses, the university had no control or oversight as to what actually went on in the classroom, specifically what proselytizing might be taking place. Since the teacher's salary was paid by the Disciples, this could influence his or her perspective and prime loyalty might be given to the church rather than to the academic institution. Furthermore, there was no tradition of academic governance or freedom, no participation in the American Association of University Professors. For example, the College trustees (mostly preachers) fired one of its best scholars and teachers for "disloyalty to the Dean," giving him only ninety days notice (university faculty are always given a year or more) and no opportunity for an investigation by the A.A.U.P. or hearing by his academic peers at the university.

As indicated previously, I had not only teaching and faculty duties but also served as the University Chaplain, a position which I held for the first ten years of my career at UGA. This position entailed such duties as general oversight of the policies and plans of the interfaith University of

Georgia Religious Association, which held program meetings each week. There was also the annual interfaith Religion in Life Week, which brought to the campus seven or eight distinguished scholars who either were specialists or just very knowledgeable in the field of religion. It was a week of discussions and speeches and required a committee of about a hundred students to work an entire year in preparation for this event. The three major faith categories in the United States at the time (Catholic, Jewish, and Protestant) were well represented among the speakers. Since a rather large number of faculty voluntarily invited the speakers to lecture in their classes (one year there were 80 speaker class visits), there was an emphasis on securing not only outstanding speakers, but speakers who might, in a general way, relate religion to certain course subjects. For example, on one such occasion we were fortunate to have the famous theologian, Paul Tillich, as a speaker. His extensive knowledge in the fields of philosophy, literature, fine arts, political and social thought (especially in Europe) was put to good use in classes in these areas.

In addition, as Chaplain I served as liaison between the university and the church student groups, trying to keep both sides informed as to respective policies, plans, and perspectives. The directors of the church students groups and I met on a regular basis once a month for a lunch sponsored by the Chaplain's office. Other activities sponsored by the Chaplain's office included a daily "sad sack lunch" and a monthly great books discussion, a Church and Community Conference for rural ministers in Georgia, and public services of various kinds. In all such activities I had the able assistance of a succession of four Assistant Chaplains, three of whom were young women with Master of Divinity degrees from distinguished schools of theology.

The 1950s and 1960s were busy and eventful years. During this time I made the decision to pursue a strictly academic career. Since a necessary condition for effectiveness in this milieu is a Ph.D. degree, I managed to secure a leave of absence during the 1954-55 and the 1957-58 academic years in order to study at Vanderbilt University Divinity School. There I was introduced to process thought by Langdon Gilkey and Nels Ferre. There I studied with the distinguished Biblical scholar, Philip Hyatt. There I had Roger Shinn as a teacher and thesis advisor. Shinn had been a student of Reinhold Neibuhr and later was to occupy his chair of Christian Ethics at Union Theological Seminary. I was awarded the degree in the summer of 1958.

Several events from those early years <u>which possessed an aura of crisis stand out in my memory</u>. During the fall of my second year at UGA, a barbecue for members of the state legislature was held in the old Woodruff Hall just prior to the annual Georgia-Georgia Tech rivalry football game, and faculty were encouraged to attend. When President Aderhold sent for me before the meal, I thought perhaps he wanted me to give an invocation, which would have made sense seeing as I was Chaplain and I gave invocations before many meetings, but, on this occasion, that was not the case. This time, a young Billy Graham was holding one of his crusades in Atlanta, and various political figures (some of whom were ardent segregationists) were invited to sit on the platform during the services. At the barbecue a member of the state legislature was pressuring President Aderhold to invite Graham to address our university community, much as he had when invited to do so at the behest of the president of Clemson. It was obvious that Dr. Aderhold was reluctant to do this, and had indicated to the legislator that I would be the proper person to issue such as invitation. Most people call this, "passing the buck."

This caught me by surprise. I didn't have time to think carefully about my response. My "off the cuff" answer was that, since as Chaplain I was paid with state funds, it would be inappropriate for me to sponsor an evangelist who would seek to proselytize the audience for a particular religion (or sect). While we had Protestant, Catholic, and Jewish theologians and leaders in our annual Religion in Life Week, they sought to inform, not convert. Fortunately, I had been a visitor at a recent meeting of the Athens Ministerial Association when that body had voted to invite Mr. Graham to come to Athens for a service. I informed the president of this, suggested that the Association would be an appropriate sponsoring group, and strongly hinted that he might consider offering them the use of the Fine Arts Auditorium (at the time the only auditorium in Athens which could accommodate such an event). I do not know what transpired, whether Dr. Aderhold did or did not offer the auditorium or if the Graham entourage declined the invitation for whatever reason. In any case, Billy Graham never came to Athens.

In the early 1950s another crisis was precipitated by **McCarthyism** and the hysteria concerning communism, which had spread across the country. In Georgia the state legislature formulated a lengthy state security questionnaire which all state employees were required to fill out and sign before a notary. Not only was it a serious invasion of privacy, but many of its sections were contradictory and ridiculous. It contained a list of over 250 organizations (most of which were obscure), of which one was required to swear that neither he nor any of his relatives (past or present) had ever been a member. One had to swear to support the constitution of both the United States and of the state of Georgia, even though the state constitution at that time was inconsistent with that of the United States. Also, one had to swear that neither he nor any of his relatives had ever tried to overthrow the U.S. government. Most people have some relatives with whom they have never had any contact and know nothing about, and even the late, beloved, William Tate, Dean of Men and a person of great humor and considerable courage, said that he could not swear to such a statement since his granddaddy had joined with those who had done their best to overthrow the U.S. government during the War Between the States.

Another requirement of the questionnaire was to list all the organizations in which one had EVER held membership. One faculty member quipped that he had once been a member of the Boy Scouts and he wondered if the legislature would find that a subversive organization. I was relieved to find that I was not a member of any of the 250 organizations listed, but was apprehensive about having to list some of the "liberal" organizations, among which were the Athens Committee on Interracial Cooperation, the American Christian Palestine Committee, and the Christian Student Workers Conference. There was never any reaction to my responses on the questionnaire.

To the best of my knowledge, only one faculty member left UGA because of the threat of the Security Questionnaire. A member of our faculty luncheon group, he was a Latin scholar in the Classics Department and originally from the North. When he was a student he had once attended a meeting of one of the listed organizations. This wasn't quite a "black list" story, but close. In truth, the man had received an offer from another university, and while he would have preferred to stay at Georgia, the possible threat to his job security in the questionnaire led him to accept another university's offer.

The ridiculous and contradictory nature of the questionnaire was finally recognized even by those legislators who had written it, and it went through several revisions. At one point it was reduced to a teacher's loyalty oath printed on the back of the yearly contract, which had to be signed before a notary. Finally, after the "Red Threat" hysteria had subsided, it was thankfully dropped altogether.

During those early years at the university a relatively minor crisis arose from an unexpected source. The head of a department whom I had thought was a friend was incensed by the topic of a U.G.R.A. program announced on a poster placed on a bulletin board in the hall outside of his departmental office, and wrote a scathing letter to the Dean of the Arts and Sciences College, censuring the Department of Religion. The topic was the "Protestant View of Birth Control," and was one of the two programs, the other dealing with the Catholic view. In his letter, this department head indicated that he had removed the poster and was "making official my objection to the Department of Religion [sic] (in truth it was the extra-curricular Religious Association which sponsored these programs, not the Religion Department) having anything whatever to do with discussions of this kind."

The dean sent me a copy of the department head's letter, and I responded with a lengthy letter to the dean and sent a copy to the department head. I indicated that I was disappointed that the department head had not contacted me directly so that any misunderstanding might have been corrected, and that we might have a frank discussion of the issues. Furthermore, it was the students on the program committee and executive council of the University of Georgia Religious Association who determined the subjects to be discussed at the Tuesday evening meetings. They asked for the two programs on birth control in order that they might know the positions of both Catholics and Protestants on this controversial subject. Then I suggested that an institution of higher learning cannot be true to its fundamental ideals and reason for existing if it cuts off responsible discussion within the community of scholars and learners at any point.

I closed the letter by stating that the students on the executive council and publicity committee were genuinely sorry if, unknowingly, they had caused this department head any embarrassment, and, henceforth, would refrain from placing any posters on the bulletin board in the hallway of his building.

The department head never responded, but I received an encouraging letter from the Dean, in which he stated, "I see nothing against having such a program, and I think you are right in your views on the subject." He indicated that I should have no further concern about the matter.

Another minor crisis had its foundation in the fact that I was a program participant in some student interracial conferences. One was the Student Christian Movement (formerly the student Y.M.C.A. and Y.W.C.A.)

week, which met one summer in Blue Ridge, N.C. The major speaker at this conference was the distinguished president of Morehouse College, Dr. Benjamin Mays. While this conference was not specifically concerned with race relations, in attendance were students from both white and black colleges, including a few from our Religious Association who could afford to attend. Another conference for students from the state of Georgia which was specifically concerned with race relations was held the next fall during a weekend at Paine College, a black college in Augusta, Georgia. Some of our students expressed an interest in going, and accompanied us (the female Assistant Chaplain and myself) to Paine.

I had been very careful to emphasize the interracial nature of both conferences, to inform our students that at Paine they would be housed in a student dormitory, and that they must secure parental consent in order to attend either one of these conferences. As I recall, there were two sets of parents who raised rather strong objections in letters to the administration. In one case, the parents had given their child permission to attend the Blue Ridge conference, but claimed that it was only later that the true nature of the conference became clear to them. They drove to Blue Ridge and took their daughter home, disturbed that UGA had a Chaplain who did not abide by the segregation norms of the South. In the other case, the student simply did not secure her parents' permission because she knew they would not grant her permission to spend a weekend at Paine College. Somehow her parents found out, and in a telephone conversation her father had some rather harsh things to say to me personally, and later bitterly complained to the administration.

Somehow I was able to weather these attacks. Given the Supreme Court decision in 1954 (*Brown vs. Board of Education*) on school desegregation, the winds of change were about to blow in the South. I suspect the administration did not want to stir up any controversy, especially since it was well known that I had insisted that the students secure parental consent.

One of the reasons why I wished to attend the conference at Paine was to enjoy fellowship with a former classmate, W.L. Bluffton, founder of Faith Cabin Libraries in South Carolina and Georgia and now (then) Professor of Sociology at Paine, while he continued the library program for black communities. Even though much of his life story and his work in establishing Faith Cabin Libraries were portrayed in a DuPont Cavalcade of America radio program (March 13, 1951), Willie Lee Bluffton remains a largely unsung hero of the Southern revolution in race relations.

I first met Willie Lee when both of us were students at Furman. At the time he was married with two children, and, even though he had a scholarship, both he and his wife had to work in a Greenville cotton mill in order to make ends meet. Willie Lee was the soul of modesty, and it was only later, and gradually, that I learned the full story of his life.

He was born into a white rural family of very modest means, and dropped out of school in order to work with his father in a sawmill. Most days, on his way to work, he would encounter Professor Eury Simpkins, a black schoolteacher who would wave a friendly greeting and sometimes stop to chat. In these chats, Professor Simpkins soon became aware of Willie Lee's inquiring mind, lent him a book from his own small, personal library, Pilgrim's Progress, and encouraged him not only to return to high school, but also to go to college and seminary, proclaiming that one was never too old to do that. Even though, by this time, he was married, Willie Lee, with the encouragement of his father as well as Professor Simpkins, returned to high school and earned his degree. During his year in high school Willie Lee received a letter each month from "Uncle Eury" in which he enclosed a one dollar bill from his forty dollars a month paycheck, so that Willie could buy little things (pen points, ink, a blotter, pencils, paper, etc.) he would need for his schooling.

After graduating from high school, Willie Lee was forced to go back to work in a cotton mill. One day Professor Simpkins invited him to attend the dedication of a new schoolhouse for black children, and Willie Lee noticed that the bright new bookshelves were empty, for no funds were left to purchase books. As he went home, the memory of those empty bookshelves and of "Uncle Eury's" dollar greatly disturbed his conscience. What could he do? He certainly did not have enough money to buy enough books to fill those shelves, but he longed to do something. All he had in his pocket was a dime which he spent on five two-cent stamps (in those days a first-class stamp was two-cents), wrote five letters telling about "Uncle Eury," the need for books in his school, and requesting a contribution of books or of a two-cent stamp so that an appeal might be made to someone else.

The magnitude of the response of those five letters was astonishing. A white Methodist church in New York (the minister was originally from Georgia) sent hundreds of books in barrels and boxes. There were so many that the shelves of the school could not hold them all. At a meeting in the local African-American Baptist Church, it was suggested that with the trees on the school property and logs from the lands owned by local blacks, a log cabin library could be built to house the thousands of extra books. Thus was born the Faith Cabin Libraries program.

After graduation from Furman, Willie Lee went on to Crozier Theological Seminary in Philadelphia, where he earned a Master of Divinity degree and, at the same time, earned an M.A. in Sociology from the University of Pennsylvania. He then returned to the South as a member of the Sociology faculty at Paine College. During this time he continued to work with the Faith Cabin Libraries program, securing books for the increasing number of log cabin libraries built by black communities. When I visited with him at Paine, I found him in an office in a large barn-like structure which housed thousands of books from all over the country. Assisted by students, he checked all of the books to make sure they were suitable for the many libraries which had now been built.

As I recall, it was sometime after the Cavalcade of America radio program that a member of the U.G.R.A. executive council who had heard the program suggested that Professor Bluffington be invited to speak about his work at one of the regular weekly meetings of the Religious Association. He accepted the invitation, and the event was publicized on bulletin boards and in the campus newspaper. The day after the notices appeared I received a phone call from a disturbed Dean of Faculties (the second in command after the president, now called the Vice President for Instruction), insisting that a guest speaker from a black college would mean trouble for the University of Georgia. The arch segregationist and political power in the state, Roy Harris, lived in Augusta and was known to have a dislike for Paine College. I informed the dean that Professor Bluffington was a white member of the Paine faculty, had been featured on the Cavalcade of America program for his work in the Faith Cabin Libraries, and that our students had requested to have him as guest speaker in order to learn more about his program. I stated also that I did not think it would be fair to the students to cancel Professor Bluffington's visit. The visit was not canceled, and Willie Lee's speech was well received by those in attendance, and, to the best of my knowledge, there was never any trouble from on or off the campus.

As a footnote to this story about Willie Lee, I think it is further justification for the validity of "Uncle Eury's" perception of Willie Lee's ability and faith in him that, a few years later, he secured leave from Paine and earned a Ph.D. in history at the University of Georgia. It was my great pleasure to serve on his thesis (a study of certain aspects of the history of the black church in the South), reading and oral exam committees.

Sometimes during my first decade at the University there occurred an event which aptly illustrates that many people do not listen very well to what is being said, and rather only hear what they want to hear. They generally wind up misquoting what was actually said.

Occasionally I played golf with a couple of instructors in the Physical Education Department. During the summers they were responsible for conducting a seminar for public school teachers on alcohol education. One summer they requested that I give a lecture to this group concerning the use of alcoholic beverages. I did so, attempting to present an objective and brief survey of the attitudes found in various denominations and religions and of the perspective found in the Bible. With respect to the latter, I pointed out that given the conditions of the times in which the various books of the Bible were composed, it is not surprising that wine was the most common beverage, and that while the Bible had much to say about the idea of temperance, it is silent about total abstinence. It is yet another example of fundamentalist doctrine not having any link to actual Christian facts.

After I returned to my office I received a phone call from the editor of an Athens newspaper informing me that two women who had been present in class and were members of the Woman's Christian Temperance Union had been disturbed by my lecture, and had come to him requesting that he publish an article proclaiming that the University Chaplain advocated the use of alcoholic beverages. I, of course, told him that such an article would be factually incorrect and should not be published. In my lecture I had simply described objectively the fact that some religious bodies do not forbid the consumption of alcohol, that the Bible strongly advocated temperance but contains NO proof texts for advocating total abstinence, but that I, personally, thought that total abstinence was the best policy. <u>I had never said that the Bible, nor any denomination, encouraged</u> drinking alcoholic beverages. I offered to show him my lecture notes as evidence, and even told him that two faculty members were present and could further confirm the truth of my statement. It seems to me that I have gotten into the most trouble when I have told the truth.

Apparently the two women remained in the newspaper office while the editor phoned me, for later he told me that when he informed them that they had misunderstood the point and salient details of the lecture, they were incensed and stated their intention to go and see the University president. I do not know whether or not they did, but I never heard anything about it from President Aderhold, who undoubtedly would have regarded it as a "tempest in a teapot." <u>While I will have more to say about this later, perhaps here would be a good time to point out how essential academic tenure is for the pursuit and communication of objective scholarship</u>.

I mentioned earlier that as Chaplain I was invited often to open conferences on campus with an invocation. The dean of the law school at the time requested that I give a benediction as well as an invocation at legal conferences. This included the annual Law Day, attended by lawyers from all over the state. In the invocations before this group I often referred to phrases and statements from the Declaration of Independence and the Constitution. Among other things, I prayed that we would remember the Declaration's affirmation that "…all men are created equal and endowed by their Creator with certain unalienable rights," and the Constitution's insistence that freedom of speech not be abridged. One of my faculty friends wondered aloud how, in the atmosphere of the times, I could offer such prayers with impunity. Still, no one attempted to silence me, and the dean continued to request that I give invocations and benedictions.

There was one Law Day in the middle 1950s, after the Supreme Court decision on B*rown vs. Board of Education,* which I remember vividly. The event was held in the university chapel, and a gubernatorial candidate was the featured speaker. As usual I arrived a bit early, and, upon entering the main door of the chapel, I overheard a portion of a conversation between two people standing in the entranceway, one of whom was the featured speaker. What I heard him say was, "Integration is going to come, no matter what we do." Yet, later in his speech he proclaimed, "We will never give in; we will fight them in the legislature; we will fight them in the courts; and if need be, we will fight them in the streets." I was so incensed by the blatant hypocrisy of this politician that I could hardly utter the benediction.

As I was leaving the Chapel I encountered the erudite and gentle Sigmund Cohen, our distinguished professor of International Law, and a refugee from Nazi Germany. I noticed that he was very pale, and suggested to him that we walk a bit. "Bob," he said, "that was the same sort of thing I heard when the Nazis were coming to power." I told him what I had overheard the speaker say when I'd entered the Chapel. I said that, while the rhetoric of the speech was disturbing in that the speaker thought that he had to say such hyperbolic nonsense for political consumption, he was hypocritical and not nearly as fanatical as had been the Nazis. To be sure, we needed to resist such talk, but perhaps we were not in as dangerous a situation as he had been in Germany under National Socialism. I am happy to report that Professor Cohen finished out his career at UGA and remained a friend of mine.

While it is true that during the decade of the 1950s I was engaged in a number of "conflict situations," it wasn't all bad. Some of it was positive and enjoyable. As I look back, I think it's fair to say that our family was not too greatly disrupted by the two years spent in Nashville while I studied at Vanderbilt. In my job at the University of Georgia I made many good friends and established and developed a number of programs which promoted the general welfare and were personally satisfying. The meetings of the Religious Association, the annual Religion in Life Weeks, the monthly faculty religious books seminars, the daily consultations with the Assistant Chaplain, and the daily teaching of a class in religion were all generally positive experiences.

As might be expected, there were many events at UGA which were open to the public, most of which were informative and interesting. Among these were the Great Thinkers Lectures, sponsored by the Philosophy Department. In the autumn of 1956 I was invited to give one of these lectures when I had been researching for a course I was teaching in World Religions. My topic was "Buddha and Buddhism."

Also, due to the nature of my job, I was able to hold membership in and attend meetings of both the National Association of College and University Chaplains and the National Association of Biblical Instructors (which later became the American Academy of Religion). The meetings not only provided a learning experience, but also an opportunity for peer fellowship. It's always fun to share stories with the only other people who completely understand what you're going through.

During those years it was my good fortune to associate with a number of inquiring and thoughtful young minds. This is one of the great rewards of working in academia. While the Religious Association and my religion courses weren't widely popular on campus, they did attract some of the best and ablest students.

One quality student who stands out in my memory is Bob Smalley. Bob was the president of the Religious Association his senior year. He continued to participate even as he attended law school at UGA. During the year that he was president of the U.G.R.A., I was invited to present a program at another college in the state concerning the organization and substance of our Religion in Life Week. I asked Bob to accompany me and to present the main portion of the program, after which both he and I could respond to audience questions. As usual, he did a masterful job in his speech, a speech of clarity and consistency. Everyone there was enlightened. Upon finishing law school, Bob opened a law office in Griffin, Georgia, and was later elected to the state senate, where he proved very helpful to the university, especially during the tumultuous years of the integration crisis in the 1960s.

Another bright spot in the 50s was Mary Frances and my bonding with other professors and their wives. We played bridge at the homes of Charles Wilson, Professor of Botany, and Alvin Biscoe, Dean of Faculties. On some occasions, President Aderhold and his wife were present. Fortunately, I was able to avoid trumping the president's good ace when we were partners.

I was a pretty bad bridge player. Mary Frances was much better. Much of what little I did know about the game I learned from Rabbi Sam Glasner. Sam was the rabbi of the local Reform Synagogue, the director of the Hillel Foundation on campus, and was studying for a Ph.D. in Education. We became good friends, and he supported me in some of the battles yet to come. Sam invited me to participate in the annual interfaith Seder, sponsored by the Hillel Foundation, to speak at more than one meeting of B'nai B'rith, the Jewish social action organization combating prejudice, and, on one occasion, to actually preach at the Friday evening Temple service, when Sam had to be away. I never thought to add Substitute Rabbi to my resume. When I spoke at Temple I made sure, of course, that the sermon did not contain even a hint of Christology or Christian soteriology (theology concerning salvation in accepting church), but instead based it on a passage from the Old Testament prophet Amos. Sam had introduced me to the eloquent writings of the learned and devout scholar, Abraham Heschel, and I gained much insight and inspiration from his two-volume work on The Prophets, especially his contention that the prophets disclose the pathos of God for the human condition occasioned by human rebellion and sin. Also, he joined Martin Luther King, Jr. in the march to Selma.

One of the things that amazed me about Sam was the fact that, even though he held two important positions and was working for an advanced degree, he was able to find time to play bridge. Sam and his wife joined us for dinner often (Mary Frances was careful not to serve pork chops, even though Sam was reform). We played bridge. We ate at Sam's home. He was a much better bridge player than I. We literally, figuratively, and purposely bridged the religious gap that divided two historically important faiths.

Among my closest friends on the faculty were Economics Professor, Ted Smith, History Professor, Horace Montgomery, a leader in the local chapter of the American Association of University Professors, and the two members of the Philosophy faculty, Paul Pfuetze and Rubin Gotesky. Since the philosophical views to which they were personally committed were so different, the warm relationship between these two was unique. Paul was a Quaker with a Ph.D. in the Philosophy of Religion from Yale University Divinity School, while Rubin was a Unitarian humanist with a Ph.D. in Logical Positivism from New York University. With his extensive training and superior grasp of logic, Rubin did not "suffer fools gladly," and yet he was warm-hearted and had great sympathy for the poor and downtrodden, and those who suffered on account of the prejudice of others, as did Paul.

Since philosophers are generally non-conformists, questioners of the mores and practices of a society, insisting upon raising the issues of evidence and logical consistency, often they are subjected to the ire of institutional leaders and the public at large. Look at Socrates. Sometimes philosophers are not much appreciated by their colleagues, even in academia.

It was well known in the University community that Paul held "liberal" views on economic and social issues, including opposition to racial segregation, which was highly controversial in the 1950s. As long as they voiced their opinions among their peers within the University, there was not a great problem. Opponents tended to dismiss them as simply idealistic "philosophers." However, this situation was not to last, for at some time after the midpoint of the decade, Paul had sent a letter to some U.S. Congressmen in which he not only included his opposition to a proposed bill for compulsory military service (to be expected of a Quaker), but also stated that he did not agree with the Southern position on racial segregation. One of the Congressmen (not a Southerner) read the letter on the floor of the House of Representatives, and it was printed in the Congressional Record.

At the time, one of the most powerful members of Congress was from Georgia and was a proponent not only of universal military training, but also of racial segregation.

I did not know then, nor do I know now with any certainty, that there was a strict cause and effect relationship in terms of influence wielded from the Georgia members of Congress in Washington on the University Administration, and the harassment of Paul and Rubin by the Dean of the College. I do know that the harassment began after Paul's letter was printed in the Congressional Record and included the elimination of any salary raises, an increase in teaching loads, claims that routine forms were always late in being returned to the Dean's office, and the continual suggestion that Paul and Rubin would be happier elsewhere. Both had tenure, and to fire them would bring investigation and possible blacklisting by the national American Association of University Professors, which would injure the national reputation of the university. So, these measures were taken in an attempt to get them to resign.

While grave consequences result form firing tenured professors, this is not the case with respect to administrative positions. Paul could not be fired from his position as Professor of Philosophy, but he could be removed from his position as administrative head of the Philosophy Department. Thus in the fall of 1956, claiming that the Departments of Religion and Philosophy were too small to be efficient administrative units, the dean sought to combine the two, and offered me the Headship of a Department of Philosophy and Religion, even though at the time I had not finished my Ph.D. Given all that had transpired, it seemed to me that undoubtedly this was a move to punish Paul and reduce the visibility of the philosophers. However, I indicated to the dean that I would need a little time to consider the offer, and immediately had a long conversation with Paul and Rubin. Both stated that they would be happy to work with me as head of the department, but I expressed my reluctance to accept the position and indicated that I would do so only if they sincerely thought it would be of a decided advantage to them. I considered the move the dean was making as very unfair and of no advantage to them. Furthermore, the dean wanted me to take on this new responsibility gratuitously, without addition in salary or relief from my work as Chaplain. If they were agreeable, I would refuse the offer, which I did, but the dean continued his efforts to combine the departments and to secure a new head, as indicated in his letter of March 23, 1957:

Dear Bob,

In my budget conference Thursday with the Committee, I was allowed a new position in Philosophy to head up a combined department of Philosophy and Religion, beginning next year.

I believe I have talked with you about his matter several times. We do not feel that two small departments like this should continue as two administrative units. By this, we do not mean to de-emphasize the courses in religion or philosophy, but for administrative purposes we feel that we must do it this way. You will remember that you were offered the headship of such a department last fall, but declined. I know you will give the new man your wholehearted cooperation.

If you have any suggestions as to a person for this position, please communicate with me. I am going to lean heavily on you for this replacement.

Cordially yours,

-------- Dean

In spite of its cordial tone, I found this letter upsetting for several reasons. The Philosophy Department had for a long time needed additional faculty and had not been awarded new positions, but now that the dean wanted to remove Paul from the headship, he was able to secure funds for a new position. This was still part of the attempt to punish Paul, and the move to combine the departments under a new head was simply a subterfuge. Whatever justification there might be for a combined department, Paul still could have served as head. Furthermore, it was now rather obvious that the previous spring the dean had offered the position to me in an attempt to remove Paul from that position as quickly as possible and not because of my own qualifications.

On March 29, 1957, in response to the dean, I sent him a rather lengthy letter, most of which is quoted below:

Dear Dean,

Thank you for your letter of March 23rd. Yes, I remember the conversations we've had concerning setting up a combined Department of Philosophy and Religion. In principle, it seems like a good move, from a purely administrative perspective. It would help to keep 'the machinery oiled and running smoothly,' to borrow some of your language.

However, persons are not machines, and I am not at all happy about what is happening to the present staff of the Philosophy Department. It seems rather obvious that the real reason for the change and for the lack of salary increases is to punish this staff. I am somewhat surprised that this punishment is being aided and abetted by men who are leading members of churches [The dean was a long-time Sunday School teacher in a leading Athens church], and have certainly heard of Christian charity, forgiveness, and forbearance. I had hoped that time would heal old wounds, and that our organizational structure could remain pretty much the same. I firmly believe that there are some values more important than organizational efficiency.

In your letter of March 23rd, you made the following statement, 'You will recall that you were offered the headship of such a department last fall, but declined.' While this statement is true, as far as it goes, it does not present the full picture. You will remember that there was no new budget position. You asked me to assume this new position in addition to my other duties. You gave no indication that I would be relieved of my duties as Chaplain. You will recall that both Dr. Pfuetze and Dr. Gotesky indicated that they would be very happy to work with me, but that I turned down the offer because I felt that it was humanly impossible to find the time or energy to assume this new task.

It would have been a different proposition altogether had I been offered a new position entirely free from my old one. That would have been very tempting indeed. However, now that the salary for such a position is assured, no such offer has been forthcoming. All of this seems to me to be most inconsistent and contradictory. Moreover, as I indicated several times in our conversations about combining the two departments, I would be happy to work with Dr. Pfuetze as head. Our relationship has always been good, and either one of us would be happy to work under the other. There is, therefore, no <u>real</u> reason for bringing in a new head, and I want to let you know that I object to this move.

It is too bad that the lives and careers of some must be endangered by this action, perceived to protect the well-being of the University by supporting the status quo in our society. One wonders what has happened to the time-honored tradition of universities as protected communities where men and women experiment with ideas. It seems that now everyone must conform or pay a heavy penalty. Are we going the way of pre-Hitler Germany?

Surely there must be some place where we refuse to give in any farther and where we stand to render a protest.

In view of the fact that you stated in your letter that the decision for a new position in philosophy was made in your budget conference, I am sending copies of this letter to the President and Dean of Facilities.

I am grateful for the cordial and friendly relationship which I have with you and other members of the administration throughout several years, and I hope that we may be able to disagree on this issue with the same spirit of good will.

>Sincerely yours,
>Robert H. Ayers
>Chaplain"

The dean's response to my letter came by way of a telephone call in which he had a great deal to say in a rather emotionally-charged tone of voice. The gist of it was that he was incensed by my letter. While previously he had sought to protect the two departments, he would no longer stand up for them, and some "heads would roll." I vividly remember that the dean's conversation was laced with some "choice" language, words which one would not expect a Sunday School teacher to use. I wondered if mine would be the head to roll, since at the time I did not yet have tenure. It was due to a fortuitous circumstance that this did not happen, namely, the dean took a position at another college!

Several events took place during 1957-59, which made for a changed situation with respect to the departments of Philosophy and Religion. In the early spring of 1957 I had been awarded a grant from the Danforth Foundation, and secured a leave of absence from UGA for the 1957-58 academic year, in order to finish my Ph.D. at Vanderbilt. My absence apparently was one of the conditions which delayed any negotiation concerning uniting the two departments.

Of greater importance was the fact that, during the spring of 1957, the dean was being considered for an important position at another university, and was undoubtedly so busy with this matter that he did not follow through on combining the departments or recruiting a new head. His leaving was certainly a blessing for me, but I was not alone in giving thanks when he was offered and accepted a new job, leaving in the summer of 1957.

During the year I was at Vanderbilt, the assistant dean carried on the work of the dean's office, while they searched for a replacement. No major decisions were made. A new dean began work with the 1958-59 academic year, and I was back at work with my Ph.D. The new dean soon began talking to me about combining the departments. I told him what I had told his predecessor, that the faculty of both departments were all for it, and that I would be happy to work under Dr. Pfuetze or he under me.

Shortly thereafter, Paul Pfuetze announced that he was resigning to accept the position as head of the Department of Religion at Vassar College. He left in the summer of 1959. At this point, the new dean definitely offered me the headship of the new Department of Philosophy and Religion, a position which would not entail continuing as University Chaplain. He indicated to me that he would recommend that I be promoted to Associate Professor of Religion with tenure. I talked with Rubin Gotesky about the new dean's offer, and, with his approval, accepted.

In the fall of 1959, I ceased being Chaplain. The administration abolished the position altogether (a move I, of course, protested), and elevated the position of Assistant Chaplain to Director of Religious Activities. I moved out of the Chaplain's office in Memorial Hall and into the offices of the Philosophy Department, now the Philosophy and Religion Department, located in one of the oldest buildings on campus, Meigs Hall. A new phase of my career at the University of Georgia had begun, a career which would be completely devoted to academic pursuits, such as teaching, research, writing, and related faculty concerns.

Bob in regalia

CHAPTER FIVE

THE UNIVERSITY OF GEORGIA, THE LATER YEARS: 1960-1970

"Let the governor of this state, its law enforcement officials and the people know that we, members of the faculty of this great institution, will not retreat from the responsibility of standing steadfastly by the rules of law and morality."
(excerpt from the open letter from the UGA faculty member detailing their decision to support the racial integration of the campus, following a racist student riot)

My new job as Head of the Department of Philosophy and Religion relieved me of involvement in extra-curricular activities, but it entailed additional administrative responsibilities and an increase in my teaching load. The academic year of 1959-1960 was one in which I had to work long hours in order to adequately discharge my duties. My teaching load involved two five-hour courses a quarter (we were on the quarter system back then), which meant ten hours in class each week. Not only did I teach a course in religion, but also, due to the pressure of student enrollment, I was required to teach one section of "Introduction to Philosophy." My philosophy major in college was somewhat helpful, but, since I had not seriously studied philosophy for some years, I had to do a considerable amount of reviewing in preparation for class lectures and discussions. My colleague, Rubin Gotesky, was of great help in this, suggesting texts and course content. Indeed, his counsel on this, as well as other matters, was invaluable.

The difficulties associated with discharging our academic responsibilities were compounded by virtue of the fact that our physical surroundings left much to be desired. Along with the Psychology Department, the Philosophy and Religion Department was squeezed into one of the oldest and smallest buildings on campus. Our offices on the second (top) floor were small and hard to keep clean. Furthermore, the Psychology Department kept its experimental dogs in the basement, located under the classrooms. Often, the first floor was permeated with, let's just say an unpleasant odor, and many times (especially in the large lecture hall) the noise from the loud barking of the dogs interrupted lectures and made it difficult to hear what was being said in discussion periods. It seemed to me that the dogs got louder whenever I had a class in that room.

In addition to Rubin Gotesky and me, there was one other faculty member in our small, new department for the 1959-1960 academic year. During the summer we had managed to secure the services of a young Ph.D. from the University of Virginia, Arnold Levinson. He and Rubin each taught three philosophy courses a quarter. Since the "Introduction to Philosophy" was listed as one of the courses to fulfill a 15-hours Social Studies requirement, each of us had to teach a section of this course. Also, the philosophers had to teach sections of "Logic," since it served as a course to fulfill a Mathematics requirement.

One of the ways we sought to meet the pressure of increasing student enrollment was to seek a possible loan from other departments of philosophically competent faculty for the teaching of one course in our field. By an arrangement with the Dean of the College of Education, we were able to secure Dr. George Newsome, head of the Department of Philosophy of Education, to teach one section a quarter of "Introduction to Philosophy." In addition, we were able to cross-list our "Aesthetics" with the Art Department, and this class was taught by Dr. Erwin Breithaupt.

During the winter quarter of my first year as head of the department, there occurred an event which illustrates how easy misleading impressions of people and institutions can spread, even if those impressions aren't based on fact, rather on mistaken perceptions, or even outright lies. One Saturday morning I was in my office, working on lectures for the next week, when I received a telephone call from the principal of a school in a distant town, asking to speak to the head of the Philosophy and Religion Department. I acknowledged that I was he, and the principal informed me that he was at the university for a conference, had some free time, and wished to come to my office to talk. I wondered why he would possibly want to talk to me, but told him that I was available. In about fifteen minutes he arrived and introduced himself.

My curiosity was soon satisfied when he told me a strange narrative. The daughter of a member of his School Board had been a first-year student at UGA during the fall quarter, but over the Christmas holidays had informed her parents that she did not like the university and did not wish to return because her philosophy professor used curse words in the classroom. I told the principal that it was difficult for me to believe that anyone on our faculty would use such language, and that, since students sometimes don't listen very well, there might have been some misunderstanding on her part (Little did I realize then how incredible her misunderstanding actually was.). I asked him to give me the young lady's name and his own address, stating that I would check out the matter and get back to him with my findings.

The next Monday I consulted with the other faculty members in the department and discovered that the young lady's name did not appear on any fall quarter roll. I then went to the Registrar's Office and found that her schedule did not list a course in philosophy at all. She had taken Psychology 101 and had undoubtedly confused the words "psychology" and "philosophy." I was convinced that this was the case, since, in spite of the fact that we had had PHILOSOPHY written in large letters on the door of our departmental office, we often had students enter and ask if it was the psychology office.

I told this strange story to the head of the Psychology Department, a friend of mine, and teased him about his faculty cursing in the classroom. His response was that they probably were not above doing such, but he thought it was doubtful. Later he told me that one of their graduate students had presented to the fall "Psychology 101" class a demonstration with white mice. One mouse was male and the other female, with the latter being the mother of the former. The graduate student had identified the female as "a bitch," and the male as "the son of the bitch." Assuming that the young lady in question was in the class, we assumed that she had taken these terms as curse words, and had then gone and told her parents that the professor, the <u>philosophy</u> professor, had cursed in the classroom. The whole incident did not say much about the student's aptitude for academia. I wrote the school principal, informing him of the facts and probabilities of the case, but never had a response from him. Likely, he was embarrassed about the whole affair, for it does seem likely that the cursing charge was an excuse for the real fact that the student did not want to return to the university. It's all pretty quaint, looking back, sad, but quaint.

Rubin Gotesky was invaluable to me, not only with respect to my teaching and administrating the department, but also in assisting me to expand my own intellectual horizons through an introduction to more recent developments in philosophy, such as linguistic analysis and logical positivism. Whatever criticism may be made about the latter as an adequate philosophical position, it is still true that its insistence on the issues of meaning and logical consistency is valuable, and that the use of these "tools" is needed in the expression of any system of thought. In addition to being my mentor and advisor, Rubin was a true friend. We had been friends previously, but with my acceptance of the headship of the department, this friendship grew and deepened. There was a fellowship of the spirit which transcended any differences in our theological and philosophical perspectives. Thus it was of great loss to me personally and to the university when, in my second year as head of the department, Rubin received and accepted a position with a much larger salary at another university. The department now had no senior faculty member in philosophy, but, in addition to its two part-time faculty, had to carry on its program with only an assistant professor and an instructor in philosophy.

Over the next several years one of my major concerns was the growth and development of the faculty and program of the department. It was obvious that, due to several reasons, such as a lack of understanding of the true nature of an academic program in religion and the credit course offered at the Christian College, the administration was unlikely to grant additional resources for the religion program. Therefore, I concentrated my efforts on developing the philosophy program and faculty. To that end, in the winter of 1961 I prepared a forty-page document which contained an analysis of the nature and role of the two disciplines in an academic institution, their history at the University of Georgia, and proposals for the future. I had several copies of this document bound in hard covers and sent to all the top administrators, including the President of the University. I do not know how much influence this document had, but there was growth in the philosophy program over the next several years. By the time I resigned as head in 1964 there were five full-time faculty members in philosophy, in addition to the two part-time faculty, and we had inaugurated an M.A. in the philosophy program.

One of my last official acts as head of the department in the spring of 1964 was the recruiting of Anthony Nemetz, Professor of Philosophy at Ohio State University. Tony's specialty was Greek and Medieval philosophy, an area that was much needed in our program for both undergraduate and graduate students. In addition to his extensive knowledge in these areas of philosophy, Tony had a superb sense of humor and was an unusually gifted teacher. Throughout the years, he contributed a lot to the expansion of my knowledge and to my enjoyment of life.

It seems that I was never able to avoid encountering problems with our deans. Perhaps a psychiatrist could make something of this in terms of a tendency to rebel against authority carried over from childhood. In any case, I had problems with the dean when I was the head of the department, just as I had with the previous dean when I was Chaplain.

As I recall, the major problem had to do with my attempt to recruit a distinguished philosopher who specialized in the philosophy of science, a discipline which would be most appropriate in light of the growth in the sciences and their graduate programs at UGA. This philosopher had an outstanding academic career in Germany, but when the Nazis came to power he fled to Africa, and then had been invited to come to this country as a visiting professor. A faculty member in the Department of Philosophy of a New England college was to take a sabbatical leave, and this college offered the German philosopher a temporary visiting professorship, which he accepted. The college was unable financially to offer him a permanent position, meaning that he was available for a position elsewhere when the full-time faculty member returned. One of our faculty had been informed of this fact by a friend at this college who highly praised this philosopher's research and teaching. We had a position available and were excited about the possibility of recruiting the distinguished philosopher.

At first the dean seemed to approve, and we wrote the philosopher about our interest, requesting that he send us a curriculum vitae. Indeed, negotiations had developed to the point where we had suggested the possibility of a visit to our campus when, unexpectedly, the dean stated that we were not to proceed in this matter. I was shocked by this reversal on the part of the dean and asked why he'd made such a decision. His rather weak explanation was that we should not hire someone who was not a U.S. citizen. I thought this explanation was specious and evasive, since, as I pointed out to the dean, there was a Hindu from India who was not a citizen, teaching in the Mathematics Department, and that, with time, our philosopher could become a citizen, but the dean would not change his mind. I then asked the dean if the real reason for his decision was due to some unstated and unofficial policy of a quota system when it came to hiring Jewish faculty. Of course the dean angrily denied that this was true and chided me for making such a statement. I responded that I thought it was unfair to me to have to experience the embarrassment of informing this distinguished scholar that negotiations must cease.

In other cases it was often difficult to get a straight answer from the dean. Around the department we often quoted as a joke a frequent saying of the dean's, "There's a great deal to be said for that, but on the other hand there's a great deal to be said against it." My frustration with this situation began to grow, and I came to the conclusion that I no longer wanted to serve as head of the department. A fortuitous circumstance made it easy for me to be relieved of the position. At the time, our most outstanding scholar was a young philosopher. William T. Blackstone, who was widely published and highly regarded in the philosophical community, regionally and nationally. He had received a most attractive offer from another university and was seriously considering leaving us. Earlier I had suggested to the dean that perhaps sometime in the future it might be a good idea to have a philosopher as head of the department. Thus, when I consulted with the dean about Blackstone's offer, he suggested that we might be able to counter the offer if Blackstone was appointed head. I agreed totally, and so in the Fall of 1964 Bill Blackstone became head. During approximately a decade of his able leadership the department grew to seventeen faculty members, increased its number of undergraduate majors, instituted the Ph.D. in philosophy, and enrolled more than thirty graduate students.

During the early 1960s I was elected by the Arts and Sciences faculty to a term on the University Council, the presumptive faculty legislative body for the entire university, but presided over by the President of the University of Georgia, and having other administrative officials as members. It may well be that my participation in the local chapter of the American Association of University Professors as well as my membership in the national organization led some of my colleagues in the Arts and Sciences College to conclude that I would be an independent voice representing faculty interests. My membership in these two organizations, the Council and the A.A.U.P., meant that I was more involved, in a relatively small way, in the integration "crisis" at the university than I otherwise would have been.

In January of 1961 a federal court ordered UGA to admit two black students, Charlayne Hunter and Hamilton Holmes. At that time our department had been given quarters on the top floor of the Academic building with offices overlooking Herty Drive and the lawn extending to Lumpkin and Broad streets. On the floors below us were located the Treasurer's and Registrar's offices, and during the afternoon of January 11, the two students came to register and pay their fees. I was working in my office when I heard a considerable amount of yelling, much of which consisted of taunts and racial slurs. I looked out my window and observed a crowd of students occupying the lawn and Herty Drive. While they were obviously agitated, the presence of U.S. Marshals prevented a riot, and when the two black students left the Academic building, the crowd dispersed. I assumed, perhaps naively, that with this demonstration, student resistance would end and the integration of the University of Georgia would proceed peacefully. I left the office at the usual time, did not observe any large groups of students milling about on campus, and went home to spend the evening with my family.

The next morning I learned that during the night there had been a student riot on campus. From several sources I was able to cull together a fairly accurate account of what had happened. It seems that on the evening of January 11th there was a basketball game between Georgia and arch-rival Georgia Tech, played at the now-extinct Woodruff Hall, a barn-like structure with such limited seating that students often sat on the floor right up to the court's perimeter. The game with Tech brought out a large crowd on this particular evening. It was a good game, with the score so close that the students became increasingly excited. Near the end of the game, a second before the buzzer, a Tech player shot a goal, winning the game by one point, leaving the Georgia students and fans angry and unfulfilled. They were convinced that time had expired before the shot was taken. They were incredibly frustrated by the loss. Apparently, someone, in a fit of misdirected anger, yelled, "Let's go get the n#*@@$%," and a mob of students rushed from Woodruff Hall up the hill toward Myers Hall, where a room had been provided for Charlayne Hunter (Hamilton Holmes lived off-campus, somewhere in Athens).

The ensuing riot probably would have been much worse had it not been for the courageous actions of the late academic giant, Dean William Tate, and the one or two faculty members who happened to be at the game. Certain non-students were urging the students to violence, but Tate and the faculty sought to calm the crowd, with Dean Tate gathering I.D. cards from some of the leaders, hoping that the threat of expulsion would quell the riotous teenagers. One faculty member and Dean Tate himself were both slightly injured by rocks thrown by some students. No help came from the Athens police, from state law enforcement, or even from the campus security guard. At the time, campus security was almost nonexistent, with only one "night watchman," himself an avid segregationist (Several times when I was working in my office late at night he would stop by and talk about how many couples he had caught making love in their parked cars or about "niggers" trying to integrate into white schools, his two favorite topics.). In spite of the fact that there was no help from law enforcement officials, Hunter remained secure and there were no serious injuries. However, the University administration, concerned about the future safety of the black students, "suspended" them and they left Athens, returning to their homes in Atlanta.

The next morning, January 12th, many faculty across the campus were very upset about the events of the previous evening, and were heatedly engaged in discussions as to what sort of actions the faculty should take. I called Horace Montgomery to discuss what could be done, and learned that he and some colleagues from within and outside the department were to meet at 3:00 P.M. in his office to draft a resolution condemning the riot, the failure of state authorities to preserve order, and demanding the return of Holmes and Hunter to campus. I was invited to attend this meeting, and when I arrived at 3:00 there were so many faculty members present that it was impossible for all of us to get into Horace's office. We had to move to a classroom for the meeting.

Horace presided and called for suggestions from the floor, which he wrote on the board. Soon it was obvious that there was a consensus, and Horace appointed a committee of four, with himself as chairman, to retire to his office and draft a resolution stating the group's views. Before this task was finished it was learned that a general faculty meeting had been arranged for 7:30 P.M. in the University Chapel, and that the president of the local chapter of the A.A.U.P. would preside. This solved the problem of getting the resolution before the faculty, for, as loyal A.A.U.P. members, we were confident that the president of the chapter would put Horace's presentation of the resolution on his agenda.

About 300 faculty were present at the meeting, and, upon Horace's presentation of our resolution there was a standing ovation amidst applause and cheers. With some minor wording changes, the resolution we had formulated at the afternoon meeting was adopted by a majority vote of those at the evening meeting. It read as follows:

"We, the undersigned members of the University of Georgia faculty, wish to commend the administrative authorities of the University of Georgia, especially the President, the Dean of Men, the Dean of Students, and the majority of the student body for the manner in which they have conducted themselves under the trying conditions of the past week, and we pledge our continued support to these authorities in carrying out their responsibilities under the law.

We deplore and condemn the incidents of Wednesday night, January 11, and regret that officials of the state of Georgia were unable or unwilling to protect the rights and property of the University and its students.

We also deplore and condemn the behavior of certain outside elements and those University students who regrettably joined in lawless demonstrations.

Continued incidents of this kind can only destroy the prestige of the University, result in loss of faculty, and discourage and depress the student body.

Let the governor of this state, its law enforcement officials and the people know that we, members of the faculty of this great institution, will not retreat from the responsibility of standing steadfastly by the rules of law and morality.

Believing this, we the undersigned, insist that the two suspended students be returned to their classes and that all measures necessary to the protection of students and faculty and to the preservation of orderly education be taken by appropriate state authorities."

It was estimated that 95% of those present signed this document, and that within three or four days it had been signed by over 400 faculty, a number which represented about 80% of the resident faculty. The media across the state, TV, radio, and newspapers gave considerable attention to this faculty action. All of this not only strengthened the resolve of our administration to obey the court order but also that of the friends of the University in the Legislature. There was talk among some segregationist legislators of getting the General Assembly to withhold appropriated funds, and thus force the University to close. Our former student and President of the U.G.R.A., Bob Smalley, was a member of the General Assembly, and I called him about our resolution. He assured me that he would do everything within his power to insist that the University obey the court order and to prevent the Legislature from forcing UGA to close by withholding funds.

The faculty with the signatures of 80% of the resident faculty proved helpful to University President Aderhold in his efforts to keep the University functioning normally. In a conversation with Horace Montgomery I learned that the day after the faculty meeting, January 13, President Adorhold summoned him to come to the president's office. Not sure what the president might want, Horace took his colleague, Frank Gibson, with him. When they arrived, the president showed them his desk filled with telegrams and messages urging him to close UGA. Indeed, he was in an unenviable position, caught between the court order to integrate on the one hand and the other by segregationists who, led by the arch segregationist and power broker, Roy Harris, wanted to close the University. The president expressed appreciation for the strong support of the faculty and indicated that he thought this would help him in his struggle to obey the law and keep UGA open.

A few days later (the latter part of January) the two black students returned to a relatively calm campus. Aware of the almost total lack of campus security, the local chapter of the A.A.U.P. arranged with the administration to have its members in a buddy system patrol the campus during the nighttime hours and, by telephone, to report anything suspicious to the Athens police. As I recall, I participated in this project on two occasions and had to drive around the campus on cold winter nights in a very old University station wagon that had no working heater. On one occasion my partner, Jim Green of the Business School, and I were assigned the hours of 3:00-5:00 A.M. for our patrol. Our route took us through all the campus streets and especially around Myers Hall, where Charlayne Hunter had a room. As we drove down Cedar Street by the side of Myers, we noticed parked on the sidewalk an old brown car with a gun rack in the back window. Along with the appearance of its occupants, that made it look suspicious to us, and we went to the nearest public phone to call the Athens police. The response we received from the police was laughter, for we had just reported agents of the Georgia Bureau of Investigation to the Athens police. We were somewhat relieved that finally state law enforcement officials were present to prevent disturbances on campus. The University was now peacefully integrated and was not shut down for even a single day.

At the meeting of the University Council on February 20, 1961, a motion was made and adopted that the faculty resolution of January 12 be incorporated into the Council minutes. Before adjournment, President Aderhold addressed the Council members concerning the recent developments at UGA, a portion of which is quoted below:

"I hope that no other institution has to go through the process of securing a football coach and integrating the same year. I would like to make a few comments about the latter problem and hope that these comments are made in executive session.

I want to thank all members of the faculty and administration for their cooperation and assistance in dealing with the trying problems we have faced since the beginning of this quarter. The expressions of faculty members and administrative staff have been encouraging and have helped to give us a feeling that we were doing the appropriate things in our efforts to meet and solve this very difficult problem. We have tried to face the day-to-day decisions carefully and thoughtfully. Every judgment made was in what we thought to be the best interests of the University and the faculty, students, and people of the state. I have said to the faculty on many occasions that I did not believe the University would ever be closed. Because of attempts to change the appropriations law under which we operate, we did come dangerously close to having to declare a one week holiday. All of the members of the Administrative Council were extremely helpful in this crisis and stayed in session practically all day on a Sunday.

I do not want to comment here upon any of the happenings during this period, or attempt to evaluate what was done on our part and that of others. Some would say that most of our troubles grew out of interference by the Ku Klux Klan, too many people in the field of mass media trying to get stories, inadequate police protection, inadequate planning on the part of all of us, interference on the part of citizens of the state, etc. This list could be long. I see no good to be achieved from commenting upon any of these problems. The important thing is that the University continues active in the achievement of its major purpose, that of educating students on the campus.

The many communications that have come to my desk give me a feeling that the problem has been solved to this point with sincerity and dignity. Many are saying that throughout the state and the nation the University's image has not been hurt, and most of these communications indicate an increase in prestige of the University. The problem is not completely solved and will not be for some time to come. I hope that we may continue to handle the many questions which will arise with dignity…

The cooperation of the faculty and staff in this crisis has not only helped in the solution of the problem, but it has made me grateful for the opportunity of working with so thoughtful and dedicated a group." (from my personal copy of the minutes of February 20, 1961)

I never had the privilege of teaching or meeting either Charlayne Hunter or Hamilton Holmes. Holmes majored in the sciences and Hunter in journalism. According to reports, both were outstanding students (Holmes made the highest grade ever in a science class) which was an embarrassment to those white students who had claimed that blacks were incapable of doing academic work at a university and whose grades were not as good as the two black students. Both students went on to distinguished careers in their respective fields. The late Hamilton Holmes became an outstanding surgeon in Atlanta and Charlayne Hunter-Gault, a world-renown television journalist on PBS. The two of them endowed a yearly lecture series at the University and, at a recent Commencement, Charlayne delivered the major address. I regret that I never had a chance to recount to them my story about reporting the G.B.I. to the Athens police.

Another issue which arose sometime during the 1960s, while I was a member of the University Council, did not come to as successful a conclusion as the integration issue. I have mentioned earlier that while I was University Chaplain I was invited to give invocations for all sorts of meetings on campus, including graduation ceremonies. I was aware of the pluralistic makeup of the UGA community and made sure that the prayers were general in nature, and not Christocentric. Even so, I had serious misgivings about the appropriateness of prayers at these functions, both from a practical and a theological perspective.

With the demise of the Chaplain's office, ministers, who had been either undergraduates at UGA or had some close connection with it, were invited to give the invocation at graduation. In our religiously pluralistic community most of them were inappropriately Christocentric. In one case, the minister used the invocation as an occasion to preach an actual sermon, and after about fifteen minutes the president had to literally tug on his robe to get him to bring the prayer to a close. Other meetings on campus that previously had opened with invocations simply abandoned the practice. This was not the case with football games, which a conservative athletic director insisted must be opened with prayer. Even as Chaplin I had never been invited to give these invocations, which was a great relief to me. Students from conservative religious groups were designated to give these (There seems to be an affinity between religious conservatism and football.). I had heard some of them, and they were not only sectarian, but also often filled with objectionable theology, such as the tendency to make God into a kind of cosmic bellhop.

Since many years previously my family and I had stopped attending football games, I was not aware of the fact that, in the 1960s, they were still being opened with invocations, until some of the ministers of the student religious groups on campus complained about them in conversations with me. They felt that such a practice was a corruption of prayer, turning it into a meaningless ceremony. Indeed, the Student Ministers Association voted unanimously to request that I make a motion in the University Council to the effect that the practice of having invocations at any university functions be abandoned, and that if any group so desired, a moment of silence could be substituted for the oral prayer. At the next meeting of the Council I made this motion, giving as my supporting reasons the fact that it had been requested by the ministers, that the prayers were inappropriate in a religiously pluralistic community, and that often the theology of the prayers was inadequate. In the discussion of the motion one of the deans (not of Arts and Sciences) argued that the abandonment of invocations at football games and graduation ceremonies would be a bad public relations move as far as the reputation of UGA with the people of the state. By a small majority, concern for public relations won out over concern for religious tolerance and genuine prayer. The practice of beginning these events with invocations continued.

During the 1960s I often found it necessary to return to my office in the evenings in order to find time for working on projects in which I was involved. These included not only course preparations and, as mentioned earlier, plans for the department when I was Head, but also research and writing. I was a writing member of four scholarly societies, and, from time to time, had papers accepted for their yearly programs. During this time, thirteen of my articles were accepted for publication in refereed journals such as The Canadian Journal of Theology. I served as president of the Georgia Philosophical Society (1962-63), the Southeastern Section of the American Academy of Religion (1964-65), the Southeastern Section of the Philosophy of Education Society (1964-65), The Philosophy of Religion Society (1969-70), and the University chapter of the A.A.U.P. (1968-69).

The late 1950s and early 1960s was a time of changes, not only in the direction of my professional life, but also in our family's church relationships. When we first came to Athens we joined the First Baptist Church, and Mary Frances and I taught Sunday School classes. At some point, my class of young adults expressed dissatisfaction with the literature from the Sunday School Board and requested that I lead them in a study of the teachings of Jesus, using a college-level textbook. We were able to secure a good book by a New Testament scholar and were well on the way in our study when the minister learned about it and objected on the grounds that it would prevent the class from following the eight-point record system, because the members of the class were not studying the lessons in their Sunday School Board quarterlies. For him, record keeping was more important than learning, and he chided me for acceding to the class' request and departing from using the authorized literature. In addition to this, Mary Frances had a distressing experience when the Assistant Minister came into the class of children she was teaching and threatened them with hell if they did not "confess Christ" in the revival which was soon to begin.

These are the reasons why we eventually left the First Baptist Church and joined in the movement to establish a new Baptist church in the Five Points area. The members of this movement were able to rent a fine old home, where the fire station is now located, where services could be held until such time as they were able to move to the present site of the Milledge Avenue Baptist Church. I was able to be of some help, conducting some of the services myself.

In order to establish a church it is necessary to have an organizational structure, so the congregation elected a Board of Deacons, and I was given the responsibility of conducting the service of installation and presenting the charge. A portion of what I said in the charge is quoted below:

"It is my duty in this charge to remind you of the seriousness of the task to which you have been called and the sanctity of the office to which you are now being consecrated. The deacon as we learn of him in early Christian literature such as 1 Timothy, the Didache, and the letter of Clement of Rome usually was mentioned alongside of the <u>episkopos</u> or bishop, and appears to have been his assistant in the conduct of the Eucharist or Lord's Supper, the ordering of discipline or establishing of doctrine, and the organization and distribution of alms. AS with the bishop, the deacon's function was that of service, as the literal meaning of the Greek <u>diakonos</u> clearly indicates.

"In 1 Timothy 3:8-13 it is emphasized that to fulfill his function of service, the deacon must achieve excellence in three dimensions of life, namely, the moral, the spiritual and the intellectual. While we may separate these three for purposes of analysis, they cannot be separated in actual living, for they are so interwoven that failure in one brings failure in the others.

"1 Timothy was written partly as a reaction to an early heresy known as Gnosticism which would have destroyed the human side of the incarnation, and thus eliminated the historical character of the Christian revelation. The author of Timothy exhorts the deacon, 'to maintain the divine truth of the faith with a pure conscience.' (1 Timothy 3:9, Moffat's translation). That is to say, the deacon should give attention to the purity of his or her intellectual grasp of the meaning of the faith.

"During the first few months of our church life I have made a mental note of the expressions of what seem to me to be some serious errors in doctrine and history. In one case the idea expressed bordered on the Hindu concept of Karma rather than the Christian doctrine of God's free grace, in another the Stoic view of a pantheistic God rather than the Christian concept of a personal God who is both beyond and within the historical process, and in a third the Gnostic belief in a manless Jesus Christ rather than in one who was both God and man. However we might respect the other religions in which these beliefs are held, when they are innocently paraded as Christian the purity of the faith is corrupted and harm is done.

"Mistakes in thought, of course, do not separate one from the reception of God's grace. The forgiving mercy of God is not dependent upon correct ideas. Yet Church leaders who are charged with the responsibility of maintaining the truth of the faith should avoid such mistakes and really work at becoming lay theologians. In so doing they strengthen the witness of the church in our contemporary culture.

"Maintaining the truth of the faith with a pure conscience leads to a deepening of spiritual sensitivity and a more perceptive moral awareness. (1 Timothy 3:8, 10, 12, 13) The deacon strives to incorporate in his or her own life the love of God as revealed in Jesus Christ, to live by the highest moral values in his or her own personal life, and to assist the pastor in leading the church to incorporate Christian love in all its relationships with the so-called secular world.

"Therefore I challenge you to accept the intellectual, spiritual, and moral responsibilities of the high office of deacon, and thus assist this congregation to be a genuine church in all of its relationships."

Later, before a minister had been called, I was invited to attend a meeting of the officials of the church. At this meeting a number of business items were discussed, such as the budget and prospects for securing a minister. As I recall, I suggested that a weekend retreat for the whole congregation away from Athens might be useful in arriving at an enlarged vision of the church's nature, mission, and function, and in determining the qualifications of a minister who could lead the church in fulfilling its mission. This suggestion received little response; instead, some of those present began to discuss the possible availability and suitability of the Director of the Baptist Student Union on campus, who was an ordained minister.

Eventually this person became the minister of the church. Not long after he accepted this position he came to my office at school. I thought that perhaps he wanted to discuss some aspect of the church's life with me, but this was not the case. Instead, he informed me that he was aware of what I had done with the Sunday School class at the First Baptist Church, and that he did not want a similar event in "his" church. I do not remember his exact words, but he concluded by saying, in effect, that he did not want me to speak in the church. When officers for the Sunday School were selected, I was elected assistant to the superintendent, which meant that each Sunday I went around to the various departments and classes, collecting records. Thus, at no point did I have an opportunity to use my theological training in contributing to the life of the church.

Sometime in the early 1960s we decided to change churches once again, but this time to a church of another denomination. During our stay in Nashville we had attended some services in a "low" Episcopal Church and found the worship and sermon inspiring. When we returned to Athens, Mary Frances and I discussed at some length the possibility of joining the Episcopal Church. We raised the issue with the children who were not adverse to such a move but had a number of questions about the Episcopal Church, some of which we could not answer. I suggested that we request the Reverend Mr. Earl Gilbreath, rector of the Emmanuel Episcopal Church in Athens, to spend an evening with us so that we might seek answers to our questions about the church. Our son, Jeremy, who was about twelve at the time, responded to this suggestion with a humorous remark, "Yea, Dad, then we would know what we were getting ourselves in for." Mr. Gilbreath had a good sense of humor, and when I told him about Jerry's remark, laughed heartedly. He did visit with us, and we did join Emmanuel.

For the most part, our experience in the Episcopal Church was a positive one. Mr. Gilbreath's sermons were always thoughtful and theologically sound. Our daughter, Sandra, sang in the church choir, and her wedding to Jimmy Holton of Camilla, Georgia, was held in the church with Mr. Gilbreath conducting the service. Furthermore, Mr. Gilbreath was of great support to us when, because of his religious conviction (much of which came from the influence of his mother), Jerry felt he must register for the draft as a conscientious objector. At that time, the head of the Clarke County Selective Service Board was under the misapprehension that the law permitted only members of historically pacifist churches (such as the Quakers) to be granted C.O. status. I sent a copy of the selective service law to the draft board. It clearly indicated that C.O. status could be granted solely based on an individual's personal religious convictions. Mr. Gilbreath assisted Jerry in joining the national organization in the church known as the Episcopal Peace Fellowship, and then wrote a letter to the board in which he pointed out that while the Episcopal Church was not an historically pacifist church, it did in its national publications proclaim pacifism to be a position which should be honored as Christian and gave his stamp of approval to the Episcopal Peace Fellowship. Since Jerry had been a pacifist from childhood and was a member of this Fellowship, Mr. Gilbreath concluded that he should be granted C.O. status. Jerry was granted such a status, and I am convinced that Mr. Gilbreath made an important contribution in the achievement of this outcome.

In many ways Earl Gilbreath was a "free spirit." I recall that on one occasion in our instruction or confirmation class someone asked him what recourse one would have if, in moving to another city, there was no "low" church, but only a "high" church available (Emmanuel was "low"). His answer was that if they were uncomfortable in the "high" church, they might consider joining the Presbyterian Church.

Even though Earl was somewhat older than I and not too far from retirement, I found his personality and theology to be congenial with mine. To an extent, it was due to the fact that he was nearing retirement age and had no clergymen to assist him, I went through the process leading up to my ordination as a Perpetual Deacon. In the Episcopal Church the deacon is a lower order of the ministry, a sort of intern period before one seeks ordination to the priesthood. He may assist the priest in many ways, such as with the celebration of communion and the conducting of and preaching at morning prayer, but he may not celebrate communion or conduct wedding ceremonies by himself. The order of <u>perpetual</u> deacon is for one who will not seek to become a priest. This position seemed to be suitable for me, given my commitment to and full-time job of teaching, but also my desire to be of some assistance to Earl beyond that which was possible for the ordinary layperson.

I appreciated the fact that Earl did not expect me to engage in as much activity in the church as a full-time assistant minister would be expected to do. He was well aware that I spent long hours in my work at the university, and only had his secretary call me when he needed some assistance in the Sunday service. On very rare occasions I preached at morning prayer, but most often I assisted in the celebration of holy communion. Not only did I gain a positive experience from these activities, but also the fellowship with Earl Gilbreath was of great benefit to me in terms of personal enjoyment and enrichment.

I was very happy in this situation and relationship for a number of years. Then quite by accident I learned that a rumor had arisen among a few (I never knew how many) members of the congregation to the effect that I was seeking to oust Mr. Gilbreath and take over his position as rector. I was surprised, shocked, and saddened that <u>anyone</u> could believe such to be the case. I could not imagine how such a rumor could have gotten started, for I had no desire to leave my teaching job to become the minister of a church. Furthermore, it was difficult to believe that those who started the rumor did not know that a <u>perpetual deacon</u> could not become a priest and serve as the rector of a church, and that only a priest could be appointed the rector of a church, and even he had to have the approval of the bishop. I was puzzled as to what the motive might be on the part of the few who had started the rumor. Did they wish to cause friction between Earl Gilbreath and me, and, if so, why? Given my high regard for Earl and my desire to keep his high regard for me, I felt that I needed to do something to put an end to such a rumor. Since I did not know who had started the rumor or had heard of it and could not set them straight, the only thing I could do at the time was to inform some trustworthy friends in the church about the absurdity of the rumor and ask them to take every opportunity to stifle it by pointing out how false and absurd it was. Apparently this did some good, for I heard no more about it, and from time to time I continued to assist Earl at Emmanuel until his retirement some years later.

Earl's successor as rector of Emmanuel was a young man who was not as thoughtful or theologically sound as Earl, but who was very energetic and active. Obviously ambitious, he naturally was concerned about the growth of the congregation and expansion of the church's programs. Soon it became clear to me that he wished to use me as though I were a full-time assistant minister. He wanted me to participate in every service on Sunday, including the 8:00 A.M. communion and the 11:00 A.M. morning prayer as well as in meetings of various church groups during the week. This was simply more than I could do. As I indicated above, in the late 1960s I was hard at work at the University with my teaching, research, and writing. I wished to be appointed to the graduate faculty and promoted to the rank of full professor. The realization of these goals (achieved in 1968) required much research which resulted in publications, and this cannot be done without expending a great deal of time and energy. I felt that it was physically impossible for me to work full-time at the church, and, with the bishop's approval, resigned my position as perpetual deacon.

Bob Ayers

CHAPTER SIX
ACADEMIC CAREER: 1970 - RETIREMENT

"There are cogent arguments supporting the conclusion that there is a God who is both a necessary and all-loving being, always seeking to lure His creatures into a loving universal fellowship."

The early 1970s at UGA were somewhat similar to the early 1960s, due to the fact that in both periods major national social problems left their impact on the campus. As described in the previous chapter, the social problem which affected the campus in the 60s was that of integration. In the 70s there were two social issues which received considerable attention and led to activity on campus, namely, the Vietnam War and the struggle for women's rights. They were both a part of university life in that decade, though neither of them produced as great a crisis for the University of Georgia as had integration.

My most vivid memory of campus reaction to the Vietnam War was of a candlelight vigil by hundreds of students in the North Campus quadrangle. Some of our departmental majors were involved in planning this event, and one of them who was taking my course in the Old Testament Prophets suggested that I speak at the service on the topic of what message the prophets would proclaim to America in such a situation. I accepted the assignment and wrote a brief statement in which I indicated that, just as in their own time, the prophets would condemn national self-righteousness, hypocrisy, deceit, indifference and callousness to the impoverishment, injury, and suffering of great multitudes of people not only within our own borders, but also in a land far away. In their view, God's major attribute is one of pathos, of identifying with the poor, the dispossessed, the distressed, and the suffering. He suffers for and with them, and thus cannot condone anything which produces such a result, no matter how much those who are responsible for such a result proclaim the righteousness of their cause. Thus, since God's love extends to all of His creatures, He most certainly does not approve of America's military excursion into South Vietnam.

By far the most eloquent and powerful presentation at the candlelight memorial service was given by Charles M. (Chuck) Searcy, a Vietnam veteran. Chuck had entered the University of Georgia to major in Music Education, only to be drafted and sent to South Vietnam, where he served for three years in Army Intelligence. During that time he learned the Vietnamese language and made many Vietnamese friends. After his tour of duty he returned to UGA to major in Political Science. At the candlelight service he told me that his experience in Vietnam drastically changed his view concerning the war. That was obvious in his speech, which had such powerful linguistic images that one felt almost as if he were in that war-torn country. I was convinced that this speech deserved to be made available to a wider audience than just those present at the service, and with Chuck's permission. I sent a copy to the ecumenical journal, *The Christian Century*. It was accepted and published in an issue during the summer of 1971, under the title, "I Remember Vietnam."

This speech provides as clear a picture of this tragic episode and era in American history as anything I have ever read, and so below I am quoting from my personal copy some excerpts which give the "flavor" or sense of the whole:

"Tonight, I would like to share some reminiscences with you, as my thoughts go back to Vietnam: back to that tiny sliver of land in Southeast

Asia where rolling mountains melt into lush jungle forests, where meandering rivers wind their ways through fertile deltas and merge with the sea; back to the gentle sunshine and the sometimes oppressive heat, the cool evenings and the muggy nights, the ubiquitous monsoons, or the days of cloudless blue skies; back to the city, back to Saigon, the pearl of the Orient, a city of warmth and beauty and vibrancy, a city reflecting the influence of the French and the proud, refined culture of the Vietnamese, a city teeming with people…

"I think of the long, tree-shaded boulevards, the flower stands along the way, the fountains, the statues, and the grassy mall along the river. And I think of the large villas surrounded by high walls, and the smooth streets which lead across the river to shacks and hovels made of cardboard and in scraps and bits of string, where the refugees live…I see the bewilderment in the people's eyes as they try to make a new life in a city which is already bursting with humanity. I see the overcrowded orphanages, the children's faces questioning, trusting, pleading, hungry for food, starving for affection, and I see the disease and the torment and the loneliness in those places.

"I see the Americans…thousands of Americans, rushing through the streets in jeeps and trucks, their rifles bristling, their eyes watchful; Americans in the best hotels, eating the best food, enjoying the best entertainment. I see air-conditioners protruding through hotel windows and Vietnamese maids sweeping the balconies with straw brooms. I see Americans struggling to carry refrigerators, tape recorders, stereos, television sets from the PX to a waiting taxicab, parked beside a Vietnamese amputee who holds out his crushed camouflage cap for money…And I see the MACV headquarters building nearby (Pentagon East), air-conditioned, climate-controlled, with plexiglass windows designed to withstand the percussive effects of rockets, with gleaming corridors of polished tile floors where Vietnamese peasants work day after day, scrubbing and shining…I think of the American Embassy: a showplace of American determination in Southeast Asia; the modern, multi-million dollar structure where the ambassador carried out his important functions behind imported teakwood doors, surrounded by lush carpets and handsome paneling; the symbol of America's wealth in an impoverished land.

"Tonight, as I see the candles flickering here in the darkness, I think of those nights on the edge of Saigon when I stood guard duty and watched flares drift to earth…I think of that night in 1968 when fighting erupted in Saigon, when the Viet Cong made a desperate attempt to drive the Americans from the cities…I remember the streams of refugees pouring up the narrow streets, burdened with all the belongings they could carry, some crying, some running, stumbling, fleeing their burning homes…moving first in one direction, then massing in another, with nowhere to go. I remember an American soldier gritting his teeth in anguish and saying, 'It's madness, sheer madness. What in God's name are we doing here?' And I shook my head in frustration and bitterness and anger and I couldn't answer…

"I remember the voice of a Vietnamese army veteran who told me, 'Vietnamese can make peace. Vietnamese know how to talk to Vietnamese. But Americans don't want peace.'

"Tonight, I think of the Vietnamese, the scores of friends who lost home and family, the ones who were separated from their loved ones. I think of the friend whose home was destroyed by American helicopters, who lost all his possessions – and almost lost his spirit – the one who could not afford to feed his children and so sent his baby to an orphanage, refusing, with tears in his eyes, our offers of assistance.

"I think of American buddies who were killed, and how it didn't seem real. I never got used to walking by a friend's bunk and finding someone else sleeping there.

"And tonight I remember the bitter statement Ong Long made to me. His eyes were moist and his lower lip trembled when he said to me, 'The American people have done so much for Vietnam; now I wish you would do us one last favor and drop an atomic bomb on Vietnam and kill everybody. Then we would have no more problems.'

"Tonight, I don't know if Ong Long is dead or alive. My last three letters have gone unanswered. I don't know about Co Hua and Ba Ly and Ong Diep and Ong Tri and all the others; I don't know whether they are dead or alive. But I do know that 300,000 Vietnamese civilians are dead because of this war. And I do know that 100,000 Americans have been wounded, disfigured, maimed, scarred for life by this war. And I do know that some of my friends, and some of your friends, and 40,000 other young Americans are dead because of this war; and they won't come back – ever. And I ask myself, "Why?" and there's no answer.

"It is for those – the ones who have died – that we are gathered here tonight. It is for those who have suffered the cruelty and brutality of war that we join together in an expression of sorrow for the shameful role our country has played in this tragedy. And by our all-night vigil here on the University of Georgia campus – safe from rockets, safe from grenades, safe from the gnawing fear that is Vietnam – let us renew the bonds of brotherhood between ourselves and the Americans and Vietnamese who tonight, 12,000 miles away, are subjected to the terrors and inhumanities of war. By this action, let us rededicate ourselves to the task of ending this war, and let us pledge tonight that our efforts will not cease until every American soldier is returned home from Vietnam, and the Vietnamese people are freed from our tragic interference and permitted to live in peace, and dignity, and hope."

After graduating from the University, Chuck lived in Athens and became involved in the publication of a new weekly newspaper which, as long as he and a colleague were publishers, took a rather progressive stance on social and political issues. Occasionally our paths would cross and I always found our conversations enlightening and stimulating. Later, he became more directly involved in politics and, I think, went to Washington on the staff of a Democratic office holder or aspirant to office. I have not seen him in several years.

As indicated above, the other issue which brought about some action on the campus in the early 1970s was that of women's rights. A rather large number of female students began to feel it unfair that the university had regulations for them which did not apply to male students. They felt that there should be one set of rules which applied equally to the men and the women.

An Honors student of mine, Kathy Omelanuk (now Kathy Agar), was involved in a leadership role in a campus woman's organization, the purpose of which was to bring about changes in the rules governing women students. Since she did tutorials with me, she was in my office for consultation several times a week. Given the fact that the subject of her tutorials was the thoughts of Reinhold Niebuhr, the theologian of Christian Realism and Social Action, it was only natural that she should talk with me about the problems, plans, and actions of this women's organization, of which she was the president. One of the problems she encountered was that members of the SDS (Students for a Democratic Society), an extreme left-wing radical organization made up of mostly males, would come to meetings of her group and try to take them over. SDS claimed to hold to the ideal of participatory democracy, where everybody had an equal voice, and yet those who attended Kathy's meetings would attempt to shout down anyone who disagreed with them.

Somehow, Kathy managed to isolate and control the SDS group and promote a rally of female students on campus. This rather large rally was held in front of the Academic Building, and there were speeches by several of the young women and even a few of the administrators. The result was a change in the rules governing female students. Kathy achieved what she had set out to do and struck a blow for the cause of gender equality, and did so in spite of her long odds, especially in the Deep South. It was quite an impressive feat for such a young woman.

I think it is rather interesting that Kathy's experience with the woman's movement, the SDS, and the reading of Reinhold Niebuhr motivated her to write an Honor's thesis on the subject, "Reinhold Niebuhr and Herbert Marcuse: A Dialogue on Freedom." In it she argued for Niebuhr's position that, given the sin of man, both persuasion and compulsion are required to bring about social change – that this is a more realistic position than that of Marcuse (the hero of the SDS), for whom freedom is little more than license. Her thesis was well-received by the Honors Council, some of whom judged its quality to be on the level of an MA thesis (Masters' level).

As I look back on it now, it seems to me that Kathy was representative of a growing number of students (though still a minority) who rejected the typical Southern mores. For example, she had no problem eating meals with black students. I recall telling her about a young black man who was a good student in my course, "Introduction to Western Religion." From my conversations with him, I learned that he was the first black who sought to play football for the University of Georgia, but that he had not been awarded any financial assistance, nor had he been given a room in the athletic dorm, or even permitted to eat at the training table with the other athletes. Having meager funds, he ate many meals in his own dorm room, using many dietary supplements. I indicated that I had already talked with Mrs. Ayers about the possibility of having him, along with some other students, over for dinner some evening. We did have dinner with the black football player, another black student (a young woman) from my class, and Kathy. Needless to say, we prepared a lot of food for the growing young people, but the students seemed to enjoy the get-together as much as the food, and the entire evening was spent in lively conversation.

While the philosophy wing of our department expanded considerably during the late 1960s and early 1970s in terms of faculty, student enrollment, and graduate programs (a Ph.D. program in philosophy), the growth in religion was considerably smaller, due to the fact that there were only three of us teaching in this field. Dr. William Power had been added to the religion faculty in 1968, and by fortuitous circumstance, Dr. George Howard, a biblical scholar with expertise in the biblical languages but teaching in the Classics Department was, upon request, transferred by the dean of the college to our department. Also by this time religion had been added to the list of courses which could be taken to fulfill a general area requirement in the Arts and Sciences College, and also in several other schools and colleges in the university. Thus, every term our courses were over-enrolled and we were forced to turn students away. In spite of the fact that the number of our majors was increasing and that we had an increasing number of students who wished to do an MA in religion, we were unable, when it came to securing additional faculty, to compete with the larger program in philosophy with its Ph.D., its needs, and its larger staff.

During the early 1970s it became increasingly clear to the three of us in the religion faculty of the department that our program could expand significantly only if we had a separate department. I knew, through my informal conversations with Professor Blackstone, Head of the Philosophy and Religion Department, that in principle he approved of having a separate Department of Religion. Thus, early in 1971 William Power, George Howard and I began to work preparing a formal proposal, which we submitted to Professor Blackstone on May 11th. In this document we included such items as a statement from the Association of American Colleges on "Religion as an Academic Discipline," a history of the religion program at the university, and a survey of enrollment figures which demonstrated the need for the addition of two faculty members in religion. There was a request that with the addition of two faculty members "Religion" be granted departmental status, a comparison of our program with that in several other state universities, all of which had separate departments with programs considerably larger than ours, and a description of what we considered to be a first-rate academic program in religion.

After several conversations with us, and a unanimous vote of approval by the faculty of the entire department, Professor Blackstone submitted our proposal to Dr. H. Boyd McWhorter, who at the time was Dean of the College of Arts and Sciences. In his cover letter Professor Blackstone wrote the following:

"For several years now I have been informally discussing with Dr. Bob Ayers, our senior Faculty Member in Religion, the possibility that Religion might develop into a separate academic department. As you know these departments are generally separate ones, and both disciplines are generally in a healthier state when functioning as separate departments. Of course we have had only two faculty members in Religion until George Howard was transferred from Classics. And even with three it may not make very much administrative sense to have a separate Religion Department.

"The proposal, formulated by Dr. Ayers, Dr. Power, and Dr. Howard, in consultation with me, requests two additional faculty members in Religion. If such can be provided, then a five-man department might be a viable academic unit.

"After you have had the opportunity to look at and react to this 'package proposal,' I would appreciate it if you could talk with Bob Ayers and me about it."

We did have a consultation with Dean McWhorter (a superior administrator) who had a positive perspective about our proposal. He was unable to grant us funds for hiring two new faculty members for the next fall, but did grant us one new position, promised us the second position for the following year, and suggested that in the meantime we formulate and gain approval from the Graduate School for an MA in Religion. With that accomplished, he would recommend separate department status for Religion to the Executive Committee of the College.

We did secure one additional faculty member, Dr. George Boyd (later Head of the Religion Department at Northwestern), a scholar in World Religions with a specialty in Buddhism. But Dean McWhorter left UGA the next year and the other commitments he made to us were not honored by the subsequent dean. Indeed, it took several years and much struggle before we were able to add an MA in Religion and it was fourteen years later before we gained a separate Department of Religion.

During 1971 Bill Blackstone and I collaborated in putting together a volume of essays entitled, Religious Knowledge and Language, published by the University of Georgia Press. I wrote the Introduction and one of the essays on "Religious Discourse and Myth," and Bill prepared one on the topic, "The Status of God-Talk." Among other contributors were Charles Hartshorne and Thomas J.J. Altizer. Also, during the more than two decades since 1970 I presented 20 papers to meetings of scholarly societies, published 15 articles and two books, *Language, Logic and Reason in the Church Fathers* (Georg Olms Press, Hildesheim, 1979), and *Judaism and Christianity: Origin, Development, and Recent Trends* (University of America, 1983). [Years later, post-retirement, in the decades of the 1990s and the 2000s I wrote two more books: *Christian Theology in a Contemporary World* (The Edwin Mellen Press, Lewiston, 1997) and *The Bible and Contemporary Theology: The Quest for Truth and Relevance* (The Edwin Mellen Press, Lewiston, 2006).]

In most of my writings I have sought to show that, while religious faith nay transcend reason, it does not have to be in conflict with reason and/or the regularities of nature. Indeed, reason is a most useful tool in providing a rational exfoliation of the faith and in relating it to all the concerns of life. Further, I have sought to show that a knowledge of the historical development in Judaism and Christianity is required if one is to be creative in maintaining the essence of the faith while relating it meaningfully to today's culture with its scientific movement and changed perspectives. While it is irrational to reject the assured results of the sciences which yield verifiable knowledge in their respective areas, it does not follow that the methods and results of science make mechanistic determinism a necessary conclusion. Spontaneity, novelty, and creativity are present in the human realm, and to an extent in the natural order. So, while I have been critical of Biblicists and fundamentalists for their refusal to revise beliefs made untenable by modern scientific knowledge, I have been equally critical of the left-wing radical theologians, such as the deconstructionists, who deny any objective reality to God and self, reducing these realities to fleeting subjective feelings. There are cogent arguments supporting the conclusion that there is a God who is both a necessary and all-loving being, always seeking to lure His creatures into a loving universal fellowship. Modern biblical scholarship has disclosed the historical Jesus as one who in his actions and teachings made evident the loving nature of God.

Even though my entire academic career has been spent in a large state university which often tends to be impersonal, I have been fortunate enough to enjoy many warm personal relationships with many good students who enrolled in more than one of my courses. On one occasion the students in my Philosophy of Religion course, with the consent and connivance of my wife, Mary Frances, threw me a surprise party at our home. Since in that course I was occasionally so involved in presenting cogent arguments for various positions that I would forget about the time and often failed to heed the standard end of the class period, those students presented me with a Bulova alarm clock. On the base of the clock was inscribed, "With Love, Your Students, May, 1975." For the next class I took the clock and set the alarm to ring at the precise moment the period was supposed to end. To the amusement of us all, it rang at the proper time.

Previously, I have mentioned Kathy Omelanuk as one of my better students, but there were others during her time and later. Several took some of our courses that carried graduate credits and then went on to earn advanced degrees at other universities. Of these I can only name a few: Paula Nichols (Ph.D., Harvard), Bob Everett (Ph.D., Columbia), Susan Kwilecki (Ph.D., Stanford), Phillip Calloway (Ph.D., Emory), John Brackett (Ph.D., Emory), Mark Todd (M. Div., Yale – like me), David Williams (Ph.D., Hebrew Union). As I write this very line David Williams is currently teaching in UGA's Department of Religion.

Having the good fortune to work with so many excellent students who were so inspirational contributed considerably to my receiving the Sandy Beaver Award for Excellence in Teaching in 1978. Earlier in the year the trustees of the Riverside Military Academy in Gainesville, Georgia had given the university an endowment fund of 1 million dollars in honor of General Sandy Beaver, a 1903 graduate of UGA and president of the military academy for 56 years. The income from the fund was earmarked to be used to reward excellent teachers in the Franklin Arts and Sciences with a $5,000 annual salary supplement for each chosen professor. I was among the seven faculty members chosen by a 10 member committee of Arts and Sciences faculty and students for the first four-year term as Beaver Professors. Not only was there the money, but each Beaver Professor was provided with a student assistant, to be used especially in introductory courses. Among the assistants with whom I was privileged to work were Mark Todd, Annette Cook, David Williams, and Angela Marsingill.

Earlier I mentioned that we struggled for several years to gain approval for a Master's program in religion. Finally, in 1979, the Graduate School did grant its blessing, and the program was inaugurated in the fall of 1980. We then had five full-time positions and one part-time. Professor Frederick Ferre, who had replaced Professor Bowman Clarke (the successor of the late Professor Blackstone) as Head of the Department of Philosophy and Religion, had been trained in religion as well as philosophy and was also able to be of great help in our new graduate program.

I have described above the efforts made by Professor Blackstone and myself in 1971 to secure approval for the creation of a Department of Religion separate from the Department of Philosophy, and that this proposal was never actualized due to Dean McWhorter's leaving UGA. We had to wait another 12 years. However, in 1983 certain conditions converged, making it possible for us to finally separate the departments.

At that time preparation was already underway for celebrating the University of Georgia's Bicentennial. I happened to be a member of a committee whose task was to suggest programs and lecture series for the Arts and Sciences College and the sources of funding to support them. Of course, faculty members were being encouraged to contribute to the General Bicentennial Fund, for the administration wanted to use this event to raise an endowment of several million dollars.

Another condition related to my own personal situation happened around that time. I was set to celebrate my 65th birthday in February of 1984 (one year before the Bicentennial). As I served on the committee, the idea occurred to me that if I retired officially but made a commitment to work full-time for at least five years without salary from UGA, perhaps the administration could be persuaded to use the funds it would've paid me to most of the financing of a Department of Religion. During the previous years, each of the many times we had requested to separate the departments we had been told that there were no funds available. Now I would counter that argument. So, I wrote a proposal of about six pages in which, among other things, I stated that since my health was good, I had no intention of retiring, but rather would continue as a full professor of religion, drawing my university salary if the administration did not see fit to finally fulfill their commitment to establish a Department of Religion. With such a commitment I would retire officially, and the savings from my salary could be used not only to support a religion department, but also to contribute to their pet project, the Bicentennial Fund. Furthermore, I suggested that Dr. George Howard, a co-worker who had served as the Acting Head of the Department of Philosophy and Religion, and thus had administrative experience, be appointed head of the new Department of Religion. Another request was that Professor Tony Nemetz, a specialist in medieval Catholic theology, be transferred from philosophy to religion.

I submitted my proposal to the Dean of the College of Arts and Sciences in February of 1983 (one year before my 65th birthday and two years before the Bicentennial) and negotiations with the philosophy faculty and the administration followed for the next several months. After approval by the faculty and the dean, the Vice-President for Instruction recommended to the President that the two disciplines be, once and forever, separated into two distinct departments. However, a copy of my proposal of how I'd suggested that this separation be financed was not sent along with the recommendation. As summer drew near without any official notification concerning a decision, and the deadline for filing for retirement looming, I was fortunate enough to secure an appointment with President Davison. It was obvious at the very beginning of our conference that he had not been informed of my offer to give up my salary, and that he did not think it financially feasible to create a Department of Religion. When I went over a copy of my proposal with him and indicated as well an obligation to the publisher of my book, Judaism and Christianity, that I felt compelled to continue to teach, he readily agreed to recommend to the Board of Regents its acceptance as well as my appointment to a position as Emeritus Professor of Religion, assuring me that approval was virtually certain. With that assurance, I officially retired early in the fall of 1983, and by January of 1984, the Department of Philosophy was finally being separated from the Department of Religion, with Howard as Head of the Religion Department and Nemetz as a member of its faculty, giving us a total of seven faculty (one part-time) for the new department.

I was fortunate enough to count among my friends the late Tony Nemetz. I was always amazed at his prodigious knowledge and the creativity of his scholarship, not only in our informal conversations, but also by way of auditing several of his graduate seminars on such medieval thinkers as St. Augustine and Thomas Aquinas. Anything but a pedant, Tony had a tremendous sense of humor and was fond of creating witty maxims. I recall that on one occasion I jokingly accused him of having only two ideas, which he dressed up in a different language. His response was, "Happy is he who has one good idea. Blessed is he who has two good ideas. He who claims to have three is a damned liar." Later, after the creation of the Department of Religion, I told Tony that at least I could be happy, for I certainly had one good idea.

Even though my action received widespread approval among the faculty, I learned, quite by accident, that one or two had questioned it. Therefore, in November of 1983 I sent the following letter to Dean William J. Payne of the Arts and Sciences College, with copies to President Davison, the various vice-presidents, and the secretary of the Alumni Society:

"Dear Jack:

"It had occurred to me that in case anyone questioned whether my service to the University without compensation matches that which would be expected of me were I still on the University's payroll, and thus whether it is a legitimate gift in kind to the University's Bicentennial Fund, you might like to have the following information concerning my activities.

"1. As you know, I made a commitment in my proposal to teach <u>at least four courses</u> during the three quarters of each academic year for the next five years. In most of our departments this is a full-time teaching load for full professors.

"2. During the current academic year (1983-84) I am scheduled to teach <u>five</u> courses.

"3. This quarter I am teaching two courses having a total enrollment of sixty-seven (67) students.

"4. I am the advisor for two students in our religion M.A. program.

"5. I am a member of the reading and examining committee for an M.A. student in Sociology and of an advisory committee for a Ph.D. student in Sociology.

"6. This quarter I have finished a paper which has been accepted for the program at the Spring Meeting of the Southeastern American Academy of Religion, and I have submitted this paper to a journal to be considered for publication.

"7. As you know, I am serving as a member of the Arts and Sciences Bicentennial Committee.

"8. As you may or may not know, I initiated the process whereby the Southeastern American Academy of Religion and Society for Biblical Literature (always meet jointly with about 250 in attendance) were invited to meet in Athens in March of 1985 as an official Bicentennial event. Our invitation was accepted, and during the next year and a half my colleagues and I will have much to do in preparation for this event.

"The other day someone asked me if I felt any different since I retired, and my answer was no. There has not been any change in my daily activities, and I would not have it any other way. For this, and for the further development of our program in a Department of Religion, I am especially grateful to you for your support and for the major role you played in bringing this to pass.

"Sincerely,
"Bob Ayers"

Later, in November of 1983 I received the following letter from Dean Payne:

"Dear Bob:

"I'm glad to learn officially what I never doubted, that you are a busy lad, hard at your tasks, with an eye to the future and with plans afoot. If any absurd question should arise, your letter will put any doubts to rout. With gratitude for your efforts and anticipation of working with you in the years to come, I remain...

"Sincerely,
"Jack"

Over the next five years under the able leadership of George Howard, the department made steady progress and gained an increasing respect from the administration and faculty of UGA. A committee of the Graduate School reviewed the M.A. program proposal, and while it recognized the need for increased financial support for graduate assistantships and faculty, nevertheless wrote a positive evaluation of its quality. During this time I was engaged primarily in teaching, research, writing, and contributing to the department's program in any way I could.

Since for a number of years I had not been very active in non-academic pursuits, such as those of a social nature, I was somewhat surprised to be invited by the Campus Ministers Association to give the address at the Martin Luther King Jr. birthday celebration on January 15th, 1987, in the University Chapel. Certainly any contributions which I may have made to the causes for which Dr. King worked and died for were very modest indeed. What could I say to this integrated group? As I pondered this question, it occurred to me that the memories of one Southerner whose life had spanned the half-century or so during which the Old South had died and the New South had been born and grown into young adulthood might be of some value. It might help to provide us with a sense of history, with a perspective on where we were then, are now, and should be in the future.

I will not attempt here to repeat everything I said in this address, but only will summarize its main points. I began by pointing out to the audience that most of the world's great religions advocate the practice of the

"Golden Rule," and that if this were really done, racism could not survive. As everyone knew, Dr. King's own motivation grew out of his Christian faith, and his Civil Rights movement was spawned in the black Christian Church. Undoubtedly it required a charismatic leader of Dr. King's faith and stature to create and inspire a movement which was the major cause for the abolition of legalized segregation. Yet there were some forerunners, perhaps of lesser stature who, with their visions of an integrated and prosperous South, had made some small contributions, especially to changing attitudes among some people. While they were a very small minority, the role they played in the transition from the Old to the New South was not unimportant. Dr. King did not work in a vacuum. There were those in the white as well as in the black community who viewed segregation as a great social evil which should be abolished.

Among some of the forerunners who were mentioned in my speech were the people I'm about to mention. There were two white women, namely Lillian Smith, the author of Strange Fruit and an ardent opponent of segregation, and Mrs. M. E. Tilly, the courageous director of the Georgia Committee on Interracial Cooperation. There was Howard (Buck) Kester, the white executive secretary of the Fellowship of Southern Churchmen, who had suffered physical assaults (tarred and feathered and left for dead on one occasion) due to his actions for an integrated South. There was Clarence Jordan, the founder of the interracial Koinonia Christian Community which spawned the Habitat for Humanity program, but which suffered night-time drive-by shootings. There was the interracial Southern Regional Council with its journal *New South*, which brought together leaders such as Dr. Benjamin Mays, the distinguished president of Morehouse College, and Dr. Howard W. Odum, the renowned sociologist of the University of North Carolina. The SRC worked to find solutions for many of the South's racial problems. There was Professor Horace Montgomery of the University of Georgia, who mobilized the faculty to call for the return of Hamilton Holmes and Charlayne Hunter to the campus, contributing to the final integration of UGA. There was Dr. Sam Williams, Professor of Philosophy at Morehouse and Chairman of the Georgia Chapter of the N.A.A.C.P., whose life was threatened often for his efforts to integrate Georgia State University.

I could not refrain from recounting to the audience a little-known story with respect to the attempt to integrate Georgia State. It was in the

1950s and the Georgia Legislature had passed a law to the effect that anyone who applied for admission to a state college or university must have a recommendation signed by an alumnus of one of these institutions. It was thought, of course, that a black would be unable to secure such a recommendation. However, Sam Williams called Clarence Jordan, who was himself a graduate of UGA as well as the Southern Baptist Theological Seminary, and Clarence went to Atlanta to sign the applications of two young black women seeking admission to Georgia State. For this action both men were harassed even by some law enforcement officials.

Of course, the massive assault on the social structures and the injustices of segregation required a magnetic leader such as Dr. King who could mobilize a following of such size and power that the forces of repression were put into retreat. Yet we should remember those who went before.

I closed my remarks with the following:

"When I think of the witnesses and martyrs who have gone before, of Lillian Smith, Clarence Jordan, Sam Williams, Benjamin Mays, Buck Kester, Martin Luther King, and many others, I am sure that were they alive today they would be pleased that now every person, regardless of race, has an opportunity to vote, that an increasing number of competent blacks are being elected to public office and earning responsible positions in business and education, and that there is now no segregation in buses, public accommodations, hotels, schools, housing, etc. I am sure they would be pleased that in this very chapel where a scant 30 years ago a segregationist politician proclaimed, 'Not in my time, nor my children's time, nor my children's children's time will we be integrated,' the president of the university honored Hamilton Holmes and Charlayne Hunter, accepted an endowment for a Holmes-Hunter lecture series, and introduced the first lecturer, Mr. Vernon Jordan, former president of the Urban League. I am sure they would be pleased that the university's faculty and student body are integrated.

"Yet many problems with respect to race relations and the conditions under which many blacks have to live still remain. We are made aware of this by many things, among which were the recent assault on young blacks by young whites in New York, the resurgence of hate groups under a variety of names such as Aryan Brotherhood and White Patriot Party, the burning of black churches, and the attempts to scuttle Affirmative Action. Also there are the inequities with respect to the availability of jobs for blacks, especially among young persons, and the higher percentage of infant mortality among blacks than among whites.

"So even though we have come a long way, we have not actualized the kingdom of God fully on Earth with respect to this or any of the other of our great social problems. Much remains to be done. Inspired by the great heroes and martyrs of the recent past, white and black, finding our own identity in this fellowship which transcends our visible communities, surrounded by a great cloud of witnesses (to use the language of the Biblical book, Hebrews), we will work to the extent of our abilities and possibilities and with the help of God to remove the last vestiges of racism from the Earth."

By the spring of 1988 I had fulfilled my commitment to work full-time without compensation from UGA and was planning to retire quietly. Without my knowledge, George Howard managed to organize a retirement party for me. At an appointed hour I went to one of our seminar rooms for what I thought was going to be a regular departmental meeting (I almost didn't go), and was greeted by the faculty of the department, some other friends, Mary Frances, and President Charles Knapp. With the connivance of Mary Frances, George had secured a photograph of me which had been enlarged and framed. He displayed it and indicated that it was to be hung in the departmental office. President Knapp presented me with a framed copy of a proclamation from the then-governor, Joe Frank Harris, commending me on my contribution and service to the university and the state. Needless to say, I was very much moved by this expression of appreciation on the part of colleagues, friends, and university administration.

Of considerable personal satisfaction to me was the steady growth and progress of the department under the able leadership of George Howard. During his tenure as head the faculty expanded to nine full-time members, all with Ph.D. degrees, and three associated faculty from other departments such as history, anthropology, and classics. Two of the nine were able African-American scholars, one specializing in the history of Christianity, the other in New Testament studies, and both in African-American religion. Also the faculty contained, and still contains, persons of different religious traditions such as Confucian, Moslem, Jewish, and Christian, and of no particular tradition, but trained in some aspect of religious studies. The main issue, of course, is scholarly competence, not religious affiliation, but the presence of persons of different traditions tends to bring a certain non-sectarianism and variety to the department.

In 1998 George Howard, head and New Testament scholar, retired. Shortly thereafter Shanta Ratnayaka, who had been a member of the faculty for many years, teaching Eastern Religions and specializing in Buddhist Studies, also retired. While I miss the daily fellowship we had in the departmental offices, we occasionally visit in our homes, play games and talk about past and present events. George's replacement as head is the able African American scholar, Sandy Martin, specialist in the history of the African American church. Even with the retirement of the two members mentioned above, the faculty now numbers ten. Two recent additions are women, one a specialist in New Testament studies and the other in religion and literature.

Certainly it is the case that the growth in the number of faculty and the increased diversity in areas of expertise has been the cause of the growth in student enrollment at both the undergraduate and graduate levels. Consistently, the service introductory courses are full, and now there are about 45 undergraduate single majors and another 15 double majors (i.e. majoring in another subject as well as religion). There are about 20 graduate students working for the M.A. in religion, and the subjects available in which they may concentrate include the Chinese religions, (Confucianism and Taoism), the Japanese Shinto faith, Buddhism, Indian Philosophy and Religion, Semitic Languages (Arabic and Hebrew), Hebrew Bible (Old Testament), New Testament, Judaism, Islam, Christian Theology, Philosophy of Religion, History of Christianity, American and African-American Religious History, and Native American Religion.

Recently the faculty prepared and submitted to the proper authorities a proposal for adding a Ph.D. program to the offerings in the department's graduate program. Surely the developments described above justify my sense of satisfaction and joy at what has been accomplished in the Department of Religion.

The same is true also with respect to the social issue of the integration of the races and the economic progress of the South. Thirty years ago I would have found it difficult to imagine the integration of our department's faculty, and yet, as indicated above, that is now a reality. Thirty years ago I would have found it difficult to imagine the integration of my neighborhood, and yet now our next door neighbors are black (also professors at

UGA's Veterinary School), and there are two other black families living in our previously all-white neighborhood. The husband and father in one of these black families is our family physician. I am pleased with these developments, for it is a further indication that in the area of racial justice some progress has been made, and, as I said in my address at the service in honor of Dr. Martin Luther King in 1987, the sacrifices of the heroes and heroines of the past were not in vain.

I suppose it might be said that a fringe benefit of my retiring early and continuing to teach without income was that I was designated an Emeritus Professor and was able to retain my office space. I had never been able to do much work at home, but throughout the years had done research and writing in my office at the university, where there was easy access to my books and to the library. I count myself very fortunate to have an office at UGA. For one thing, I am able to maintain fellowship with colleagues, to learn of their scholarly endeavors, and to keep informed about developments in the department. Also it motivates me to continue doing some research and writing. Since actually retiring (about ten years ago) I have learned to type (previously all my writing was done long-hand), and while not an expert, I have learned to use a computer as a word processor. When the department secured new computers, George Howard gave me his old one for use in my office. It greatly facilitates the preparation of documents.

With the use of the computer I have prepared an article of some 27 pages as well as a book-length manuscript (two actually, if you count the one you are almost done reading right now). The article was published in volume 48 of the Union Seminary *Quarterly Review* and dealt with the "Ecumenical Thought of Reinhold Niebuhr." To the best of my knowledge, even with the voluminous writings on Niebuhr's theology and his well-known participation in ecumenical activities, no one had written a full-length study of his outlook on ecumenical thought. As I researched his writings to glean from them his outlook on ecumenism, I learned that it was much more inclusive than might have been thought, extending beyond Protestantism to include Catholicism, Judaism, and the other great world religions.

Niebuhr emphasized the dialectic of a genuine commitment to a particular religion combined with a genuine tolerance for all religions. In volume 2 of his *Nature and Destiny of Man* (1943), he wrote of a "hidden Christ" which operates in history, and proclaimed that there is always the possibility that those who do not know the historical revelation may achieve a more genuine humility and repentance than those who do (pp.109-110). In his introduction to his last major book, *Man's Nature and His Communities* (1965), he declared an increasing devotion to the principles of religious pluralism in an open society which allows the various religious faiths and traditions to contribute their treasures to our common fund, and concluded that only a great multitude of diverse, and sometimes contradictory, traditions can serve to illuminate the meaning and mystery of human existence.

I agree with Niebuhr's position. I, too, believe that in Jesus Christ, God is disclosed as *Agape*, the ultimate being of self-giving love. If this is so, then it follows that insofar as a church or denomination humbly accepts this conviction, it seeks to demonstrate a loving and accepting spirit to all, both to other Christian bodies and to non-Christians. Any church or denomination which rejects an ecumenical spirit and refuses to engage in ecumenical action is failing to follow the norm of *Agape*. Ecumenism is of the very essence of an authentic Christian faith.

The book-length manuscript which I have written is entitled, *Christian Theology in a Contemporary World*. I finished it quite a while ago, but it has taken a considerable amount of time for it to be considered by various publishers. In the fall of 1996 I signed a contract with the Edwin Mellen Press for its publication, and it was indeed published in March of 1997. This press published many scholarly books, which are acquired by research libraries throughout the world.

My purpose in writing this book at this late stage in my life was to bring together and discuss in a rational and systematic way the various elements of my theology. I am convinced that a rational and intelligible faith sustains the human spirit much better than one which is irrational and unintelligible. Thus, in the introduction I argue that reason is not necessarily antithetical to faith, but may be legitimately used as an essential servant in the task of faith seeking understanding. The task of the servant is to enlarge our understanding of the implicit and explicit meanings in the Christian mythos, to demonstrate that its essential affirmations are not irrational or falsified by the facts of experience, and to show their relevance to individual life and the discipline of culture. After this introductory chapter on method, I sought to raise issues of meaning and of meaningfulness and relevance in the modern world in the following areas: Human Nature and Destiny, God, Christology, Soteriology, Church, and Eschatology.

Among other things, I was concerned in this volume with the question of whether or not we can preserve the intent of the framers of the traditional doctrines of the Christian faith while eliminating some metaphysical concepts which are not viable in our world and by using different concepts. My argument is that we can do so without on the one hand going to the radical extremes of the deconstructionists who deny the objective reality of self, and on the other hand capitulating to the irrationality and absurdity of fundamentalism.

It seems obvious that the notion of the revelation of God would be vacuous without beings capable of receiving, appreciating, and to a large extent understanding that which is revealed. <u>This requires a self with the capacity for transcending to some degree the world of objects, including the body, and possessing a relative freedom</u>. So I attempt to show that there are good grounds for affirming the existence of such a self. The existence of such a self is a necessary condition for even the possibility of a relationship with God, and this relationship is a necessity if there is to be a genuine understanding of the self.

A relationship with God is dependent not only on the existence of a subject self but also on the actual existence of that being possessing the attributes generally assigned to the One we call God. Thus I argue that "belief that" is a necessary condition for "belief in," whether it be persons or God. So there should be good reasons for affirming the existence of God, and I argue that while there is no final and absolute proof, the traditional arguments for the existence of God, taken together, provide good grounds for the rationality of the belief that He does in fact exist. However, this does not tell us <u>who</u> God is, or what His evaluations of the world are. For this, revelation or God's self-disclosure are required.

It is the Christian claim that in Jesus Christ was the conclusive revelation of God, however many, various, and contradictory theories have been propounded in the history of Christian thought as to how this could be the case and/or what it means. It is my conclusion that by using the historical critical approach we can glean from the Synoptic Gospels of the New Testament the picture of one who, in the words of Dietrich Bonheoffer, was "totally in the world for others." In his life, teachings, suffering, and death, he disclosed who God is, namely, one who is *Agape* (continual self-giving love). *Agape* is inclusive and universal, and without prior conditions accepts everyone into fellowship who accepts the acceptance. Faith is the trust that, no matter how unworthy, one is accepted by a loving God on the basis of his or her acceptance of God's acceptance.

The divine fellowship is represented on Earth by the church which, with its many divisions and inadequacies, is often a rather weak vessel for the fellowship. Any church which seeks to be true to the ideal of the divine fellowship - the kingdom of God - should be at work attempting to banish the divisions, to instruct and encourage its members to know and live by the deeper meanings of the faith, and to act for the improvement of society.

Finally, in the concluding chapter on eschatology, I maintain that a theology of confident hope for the future, both in this life and the next, is an integral part of the Christian faith, but that Apocalypticism (various theories about cataclysmic endings of history and time sent by God) is <u>not</u>. If God is Agape, then He acts through the power of persuasion to lead us toward greater approximations to His kingdom while we are on Earth and ultimately into that final universal fellowship in which everyone lives with God and others in perfect freedom and faithfulness.

In addition to my continuing to do research and writing (and occasionally substitute teaching) during my retirement years, Mary Frances and I have enjoyed participating in the Elderhostel program. This is a national and international program for persons 55 years and older, and there is a national office which periodically sends its participants three catalogs listing its various available programs. Generally, each individual program is sponsored by a college or university, and over the course of a week consists of faculty lectures on three topics. Mary Frances and I have attended nine Elderhostels in different parts of the United States, and our courses have included such topics as China, the Soviet Union, the Middle East, the environment, the Amish, the Navaho culture, antiques, drama, and Southern writers.

I have found the courses to be informative and, for the most part, interesting. One which stands out in my memory was the one on Southern writers. This was the case primarily, I think, because one of the writers was Richard Wright, and in preparation for the "course" I read his novel, *Native Son*, which so clearly and powerfully reveals the plight of blacks in our country, especially prior to and during the time of the Great Depression. Surely any white person who is genuinely committed to the belief in a God of self-giving love cannot read this book without a sense of guilt, sorrow, and even indignation at the terrible oppression of blacks by whites for so many years. Of course, by means of his writing, Wright was able to struggle out of poverty and take his family to live in Paris.

This program was memorable also because I had a chance to meet Wright's daughter and hear her speak. She still lives in France, where she is a journalist, but came to Natchez, Mississippi to participate in this program. Her speech included a number of anecdotes about the relationship of her famous father with family and friends, especially in France. One such anecdote recalled that when she was about five years of age she went with her family to a dinner party in the home of a famous writer, Gertrude Stein, and was reprimanded by Stein for sitting in a small chair which contained a tapestry, the design of which had been created by Pablo Picasso. Her father defended her by chiding Stein for displaying the valuable tapestry on a small chair on which a child would be tempted to sit, and insisted that personal feelings of acceptance and worth, especially in children, are more important than property values.

Previously, I have written about the New South where there have been improvements in race relations and economic conditions, major issues in the agenda of the liberal. Yet it appears to be one of the ironies of American history that the social progress supported by and to a considerable extent brought about by liberals has been accompanied by an increase of conservatism, both socially and religiously. In some cases, progress brings a reaction which is extreme, as in groups such as the various militias where the use of force and violence is advocated. Often this is spurred on by the inflammatory rhetoric of right-wing political leaders. In our so-called enlightened times, I am somewhat bemused by these developments, even though, with my background in Reinhold Niebuhr's brand of Christian Realism which rejected the notion of <u>inevitable</u> social progress as naïve, I should not find it surprising. In human history progress is never without its attendant evils. Since every human being is a mixture of saint and sinner, possesses indeterminate possibilities for good <u>and</u> indeterminate possibilities for evil, inevitable progress, a building of the kingdom of God on Earth, is impossible. Yet we can make some progress, eliminate some evils, and improve society. Niebuhr himself worked for social reform while at the same time reminding us of the ambiguous mixture of good and evil in both individuals and societies. While he accepted the designation "Christian Realism" for his theology, he retained much from the liberal theology of his seminary training, especially the Christian's obligation to work for the improvement of society. In my judgment one can hold to a theology of Christian Realism and still accept the designation of liberal if, as I pointed out in Chapter One, this word "liberal" is understood in terms of the definition provided in standard dictionaries of the English language.

It is rather sad that in many recent political debates "liberal" is directed against opponents as though this position was something worse than being a thief or a murderer. There is never an indication of the word's meaning, but only the displaying of a negative emotive connotation which denigrates anyone who is labeled by the term.

<u>Throughout my life I have been proud of being labeled a liberal and have sought to be worthy of such a designation.</u>

I have sought to value persons more than things and to be free from bigotry and not limited by authoritarian attitudes and dogmas.

While honoring the past, I have sought to be open to new ideas, in favor of proposals for progress, and appreciative of the other great cultures of the world with their myths, their artifacts, their histories, and their great thinkers.

In addition, I have sought to avoid holding to simplistic claims and slogans and to reason correctly in terms of logic and the demands of the empirical evidence.

I would be the first to admit that I have not always been successful in these endeavors, but I think that the striving to live up to these ideals is that which defines a liberal, and that is an honorable position to hold.

THE END

A MEDITATION ABOUT THE GOD OF LOVE AND HUMAN DESTINY

Robert Ayers, Emeritus Professor of Religion, University of Georgia
(written soon after the passing of my beloved wife,
Mary Frances Cooley Ayers)

Recently, a most shocking statement was made by a famous evangelist, that Mahatma Gandhi, the non-violent pacifist hero of Indian independence, is suffering in hell because he was not a Christian. In terms of its implications for that which is real, this claim is nonsense, because it presupposes the ancient three-story universe, with hell below, earth in the middle, and heaven above. Furthermore, this kind of sectarian exclusiveness would banish the majority of humanity from God's love and concern. Those conservatives who follow this evangelist believe that only "Christians" of a certain type are "saved." Adherents of no religion or of other religions such as Hinduism, Buddhism, Confucianism, or Taoism, are lost and are in hell. Yet if God is a God of unsurpassable love, it follows that God loves everybody in the whole world and deeply desires that every human being receive and give love.

So what may be said about God, heaven, and hell that makes some kind of sense? Perhaps, a fictional and fanciful dialogue may provide some perspective.

Well, God is puzzled and asks St. Peter why Gandhi was denied admission, and turned away so as to go to hell.

"But God," says St. Peter, "this very famous evangelist told me that the position of his denomination is that hell is a real eternal conscious punishment for those who reject the Gospel and for non-Christians. He didn't mention Satan, which may have been an oversight or too much of a mythological figure for even him to believe real. However, he did say that he had preached all over the world and that resulted in the saving of thousands of souls and thus was very close to you. He definitely claimed that Gandhi's name should not be on the list of those to be accepted, since he was not a

Christian, and all non-Christians or pagans should not be on my list. He said also that there were some professing Christians that did not deserve to be there, for example Martin Luther King, who, though a great preacher and leader, went to India to visit Gandhi's birthplace, praising Gandhi and accepting his program of non-violence. I did not want to bother you, because you were very concerned about the raging conflict in Rwanda where the majority Hutu were trying to wipe out the Tutsis, and you were seeking to persuade the Hutu to stop the killing. Thinking the evangelist had your approval, I sent him away."

I'll tell you, old St. Pete, you really goofed this time.

God asked, "What's all this about 'saving souls'? That's a reflection of the ancient Gnostic heresy that claimed ultimate spiritual knowledge about an ultimate God above the God of Jesus. 'Saving souls' doesn't mean much to most people today. Furthermore, it is so overused by some evangelicals that it has pretty much become a rote saying. It might be helpful to all if they just abandoned that expression. What Christians need to do is not talk so much about being 'saved,' rather to seek to live as thinking, willing, and loving total persons. Gandhi was such a total person who sought his whole life to bring about peace. His life was more like that of our beloved Jesus than the lives of those who think he belongs in hell. I'll tell you, Pete, heaven is getting so cluttered with those pseudo-Christians that it has become almost a stuffy place, instead of one of joy and happiness."

"Oh, God, I'm so sorry I made such a mistake. If you'll forgive me, and I know You will, I'll try to do better in the future. I swear I was not responsible for this next case, at least not directly. This lovely Christian lady, Mary Cooley, came for admission, and asked where she might find Mr. Gandhi, since as a committed pacifist, she had always admired him for his lifestyle and his absolute commitment to and practice of non-violence. She said that she would very much like to meet and talk with him. I told her some of her fellow religionists were responsible for his being in hell. With that, she said, 'They are not my fellow religionists,' and off she went to find Mr. Gandhi."

"Well, St. Pete, I tell you, those pacifists are near to my heart, and I just wish the whole world were full of them."

"But God, with all Your power, why don't You arrange that?"

"Now Pete, you know better than that. You know I can't do that, for no one can be forced to be peaceful, to love. Love and peace must be voluntary or they are not genuine. Both Gandhi and Mary Cooley, out of deep concern for the human condition, voluntarily decided to be pacifists. I expect that Mary Cooley is going to be surprised when she reaches the Mahatma with the company he keeps. Of course, during her earthly life she knew that Martin Luther King admired Gandhi and followed Gandhi's principle in his struggle of gaining civil rights for all persons, regardless of race. And, I guess that King's admiration for Gandhi, plus his affirmation at 13 that he did not believe in the physical resurrection of Jesus is the reason his name is not on your list, Pete. But there will be other people there who will surprise her."

"But God," said St. Peter, "I doubt that Mary Cooley will be surprised that other Christians who share her outlook, and adherents of other religions, such as the great Jewish scholar and mystic, Abraham Heschel, were not on my list, and are present in the Gandhi fellowship."

"Yes, Pete, but I suspect that she will be surprised that our beloved Jesus is not with me in heaven, sitting on some kind of throne, but is in hell, working with those who are so full of hatred and loathing that they reject my unsurpassable love, and will not associate with the Gandhi group. Jesus is so full of my agape love that he is seeking to persuade them that I love them also, that I deeply yearn for them to change and to accept my love and live with others in this love. So far, some have changed, and are lovingly associated with Gandhi and his friends. Would that all were, but since I am AGAPE, loving persuasion wins universally. In the meantime, Pete, let's listen to Mary Cooley's and Mahatma Gandhi's conversation."

"Mr. Gandhi, I'm Mary Cooley, and I came here because I wanted to meet you, and tell you how much I've admired you for your tremendous life and work for the cause of non-violence, peace, abolition of the caste system, racial segregation, and that the success of all this requires a genuine and thorough-going morality in all the venues of society, such as politics, business, education, and entertainment."

"Thank you very much, Mary Cooley, but please, call me Mahatma. Everybody does."

"I will, Mahatma, if you will call me Mary. I am not a bit surprised that I see Martin Luther King in your group. I admire him as well for, like you, he worked for racial justice, and, like you, he was assassinated. Apparently, in the world people like you cannot be tolerated by those who are prejudiced against other races and persons who are different, and are totally convinced that everything they believe, no matter how absurd, is absolutely true simply because they believe it.

"Unfortunately, Mary, that is too often the case with too many people. Although not a Christian, I have always admired, accepted, and tried to live by Jesus' teachings. If everyone would seek to do that, they would not be full of prejudice and hatred, but instead full of love for all people no matter how different or no matter what religious tradition they came from. Next to Jesus, I have always admired St. Francis for his lifestyle and his enormous love for everything in the world of nature as well as for persons of simplicity and kindness."

"Yes, Mahatma, I have always known of your admiration for Jesus, and it is not surprising that you admire St. Francis, since there is considerable similarity in your lifestyles. I'm sure that the reason he is not here in our company is that he preceded the extreme sectarian "Christians" by many centuries, but I'm sure he has been a joy to God. If those sectarians were aware of St. Francis' outlook and not just his reputation, they would want to consign him, post mortem, to hell. As with most of the great saints and mystics, St. Francis believed that the God of unsurpassable love was the lover of all creation and the ultimate source of all religions. This is expressed so often in the beautiful poetry of the saints and mystics. One of my favorites of St. Francis is:

"I once spoke to my friend, an old squirrel, about the Sacraments---he got so excited and ran into a hollow in his tree and came back holding some acorns, an owl feather, and a ribbon he had found. And I just smiled and said, Yes, dear, you understand: everything imparts His grace."

"Oh, Mary, I can understand why that is one of your favorite St. Francis' poems, for it expresses in such a succinct but delicate way his total understanding of life and reality."

"I agree, Mahatma, but I would be pleased to hear you recite a poem from your favorite saint of India."

"Well, Mary, there are many whom I admire, but I think my favorite is Kabir, from the 15th century, for his poetry demonstrates Hindu, Muslim, and Christian influences and perspectives. He was truly ecumenical. During his lifetime he was denounced by the adherents of each tradition, as was I, but after his death he was revered as a saint. Whether or not that will be my lot or not, I don't know. It was not a goal of mine, for my concern was to create more peace in the world. The Kabir poem which speaks so powerfully to me that it brings tears to my eyes is entitled 'HOW HUMBLE IS GOD?'"

"How humble is God? God is the tree in the forest that allows itself to die and will not defend itself in front of those with the axe, not wanting to cause them shame. And God is the earth that will allow itself to be deformed by man's tools, but he cries; yes, God cries, but only in front of his closest ones. And a beautiful animal is being beaten to death, but nothing can make God break his silence to the masses and say, 'Stop, please stop, why are you doing this to me?' How humble is God? Kabir wept when I knew."

(Ladinsky, Daniel, *Love Poems from God*, Penguin Books Ltd., London, England)

"Wow, Mahatma. In spite of its pantheistic note, and we could all do with a bit of pantheism, this poem speaks so powerfully of God's grief and suffering over our world. Should not persons have empathy for God and His suffering, and not be babbling about His omnipotence, understood as His actively willing disturbances in nature in order to punish people for misdeeds, real or imagined? One of those babblers was the minister who proclaimed that the real reason for the New Orleans flood after Hurricane Katrina was God's punishment of the whole city because of the lifestyle that was prevalent among some persons there. Surely, God gave a great sigh of sorrow upon hearing that. I think that the most important thought and attitude of every human being should be to love and bring joy to God."

"I agree, Mary. It is indeed sad that some people create gods in their own images instead of trying to rid themselves of their egocentrism in order to live fully in the light of God's unsurpassable love. This is what the great saints and mystics did to a greater degree than most people. I learned so much from so many of them during my life and I can tell that you have been acquainted with some. Your attitude reminds me of the great Persian Sufi Master of the 14th century, Hafiz, who proclaimed,

"This sky where we live is no place to lose your wings, so love, love, love."
(Ladinsky, Daniel, translator, *The Gift,* Penguin Books, 1999, p.169)

"Well, here comes Jesus, Mary. Welcome to our group."

"That admonition of Hafiz, Mahatma, is one that I wish everyone followed, for then everyone would follow your policy of nonviolence and peace."

"Yes, Jesus, you are certainly correct about that. I suspect that you have come from your arduous task of seeking to persuade the wicked and depraved spirits gathered around Hitler, and the other slaughterers of history, to accept the love of God."

"That is true, Mahatma, but I wanted to spend at least a little time with your group, since you have such a similar outlook to mine. Of course, I know all the personal spirits in this group."

"As you know, Jesus, I am Mary Cooley, and I'm so glad you have joined us. I want to ask you some questions. When I was physically alive, my husband and I encountered some of your narratives in our study of the New Testament Gospels that are simply unbelievable. For example, were you really born of a virgin as the late-first century Gospels of Matthew and Luke proclaim?"

"Not so far as I know. Mary and Joseph acted as perfectly normal parents. When I began to preach, my mother and brothers came to where I was, apparently to take me home because they did not think that was something I should be doing. But would that have been the case if I had been conceived without the help of a male spouse? Would my mother have been surprised by that or by many of the other things I did or said, like my questioning the scholars and rabbis in Jerusalem when I was young if I really hadn't been her real son? I don't think so. I don't think she would have been surprised by any of the unusual things I did and said. As you know, there were opponents of early Christianity who claimed that I was the illegitimate son of Mary and either a Roman soldier or a demon or heavenly watcher. And the virgin birth stories were an attempt to claim these as false and defend my character and my mission. I'm sure they are not historically true, but they were created for apologetic reasons. Do you have any more questions, Mary?"

"Yes, Jesus. I've wondered if the Gospels, with their emphasis on a supernatural character and a Messianic role, accurately reflect your real understanding of your nature and your mission. Did you really think of yourself as supernatural and Messianic? As I recall, even in the Gospels it was other people who called you the Messiah, but it was not used by you as a self-description. Instead, you call yourself a prophet."

"That is exactly how I thought of myself, Mary, as in the tradition of the great prophets of Israel, the Nabi, or spokesmen for God."
"But, Jesus, what about your riding a donkey into Jerusalem at Passover? Some say that this reflects a Messianic passage in Zechariah?" (Zechariah 9:9)

"Well, Mary, that passage simply had to do with typical entry processions, symbolizing the king or official to be inaugurated. It reminded him, or me in this case, to remain humble. In my world, entry processions of all kinds of officials, secular and religious, were important events. They indicated that the leaders, such as a general leading a victorious army or a king or prince were so important and powerful that ordinary people must be obedient and serve them. So, I rode a donkey into Jerusalem when there were great crowds there during Passover as a caricature of such entry processions, to ridicule both the Roman and the Temple authorities. I wanted to show that humble service and love were more pleasing to God than power and control. In addition, I had to take a prophetic stand against the Temple authorities because they were cheating the people in the changing of their coins into Temple coins and in levying an excessive Temple tax. I turned over the tables of the moneychangers and accused the Temple authorities of turning the Temple into a den of robbers. Of course, the Romans were not happy with the crowds and the popular acclaim I was receiving. All they understood was physical force, warfare, and domination. They didn't understand my concern for service, peace, and love, and so they assumed that I was attempting to lead an earthly rebellion."

"Well, Jesus, it's no wonder that you were persecuted and put to death since, like the prophets of old, you opposed the powerful for the sake of the poor, the persecuted, the downtrodden, and the ordinary people of your time. You were indeed in the world totally for others, challenging the power structures. And, of course, the temple authorities and Pilate could not put up with that and had to rid the world of you. But I think the Roman governor, Pilate, who gave the order for your crucifixion, must be charged with the major responsibility for your death, in spite of the later attempts by some Christians to shift the responsibility entirely to the Jewish people. But I must not dominate the conversation, for I'm sure there are others present who would like to engage in conversation with people here of differing traditions. What do you think, Mahatma?"

"I agree, Mary, for, as you know, I have and do respect all traditions. Indeed, I am fond of the following passage from the great 14th century Persian Sufi poet, Hafiz, **"I have learned so much from God that I no longer call myself a Christian, a Hindu, a Buddhist, a Jew. The truth has shared so much of itself with me."** (*ibid*, p.32) Undoubtedly, each of us here is involved in a certain tradition and honor it, yet are not bound by it, but recognize the value in other traditions and honor them. Our conversations are certainly not limited by any time constraint, so let's begin."

"Mahatma, Mary, and Jesus, I, as you know, am Abraham Heschel, a friend of Martin Luther King, the great advocate of civil rights for all people, and who I'm pleased to note is here, and, of course, Reinhold Neibuhr, who, in my judgment, was not only America's foremost theologian, but also was among the first to understand and appreciate my thinking. Also, Mary, I believe he was your husband's favorite theologian."

"And, Mr. Heschel, my husband also thought your book on the Old Testament prophets was by far the best study of the prophets. One of our favorite devotional books was your *Man's Quest for God*, and I will attempt to quote some favored passages:

"When we begin to feel a qualm of diffidence (toward God) lest we hurt what is holy, lest we break what is whole, then we discover that He is not austere. He answers with love our trembling awe – we become sharers of gentle joy."

"To pray is to take notice of the wonder, to regain a sense of the mystery that animates all beings, the divine margin in all attainments. Prayer is our humble answer to the inconceivable surprise of living. It is all we can offer in return for the mystery by which we live."

"There are a couple of other passages from your speech on 'Religion and Race,' which meant a great deal to me, for we had opposed segregation in the early 1940s. We never had a chance to meet Dr. King, but supported his work for racial integration and for peace and were aware that you two were friends. We were delighted by the speeches both of you gave at Riverside Drive Church in New York against the Vietnam War. I'm sure Dr. King approves of the following passage from your article, 'Religion and Race':

"How can the two be uttered together? To act in the spirit of religion is to unite what lies apart, to remember that humanity as a whole is God's beloved child. To act in the spirit of race is to sunder, to slash, to dismember the flesh of living humanity. – It is a treacherous denial of the existence of God. Any god who is mine but not yours, any god concerned with me but not you is an idol. Faith in God is not

an afterlife-insurance policy. It is more concerned with the integrity of love than the purity of dogma.
(Heschel, Sussanah, *Essential Writings of Abraham Heschel*, pp.65-75)

"Mary, I am Martin Luther King, but please call me Martin. I think that article was the best thing ever written on religion and race at a time when the most segregated hour of the week was 11:00 A.M. Sunday morning."

"I definitely agree, Martin. So many ministers were afraid to speak out against the evil of segregation and their 'Christian' congregations insisted on white-only membership and visitors. One notable exception in the early 1940s was the Fellowship of Southern Churchmen, a group of younger ministers and some laity, who opposed segregation, the sharecropping system, and rejection of labor unions by the cotton mills. The opposition to this group was vicious. One leader was tarred and feathered and ridden out of his state on a rail. Several of the young ministers lost their jobs. I think that this may have been some time before you began your crusades, Martin."

"Yes, it was, Mary, but I knew about it and it was an inspiration to me as were so many supporters, such as Dr. Benjamin Mays, President of Morehouse, Dr. Reinhold (Reinie) Niebuhr and, of course, Dr. Abraham Heschel, who courageously joined me in the March to Selma."

"It is quite clear, Martin, you appreciate, as evidenced in your 'I Have a Dream' speech, that there were fore-runners who sought time and again, even if unsuccessful, to bring into fruition the promissory note in the Declaration of Independence that '**All men are created equal; that they are endowed by their Creator with certain unalienable Rights; that among these are Life, Liberty, and the pursuit of Happiness.**' If I may say so, I think your speech was one of the greatest speeches of all time. But if I may make another comment to Mr. Heschel, it seems to me that your early life experiences of Hasidism has resulted in an understanding which is similar to many of the great mystic poets of several religious traditions who were convinced that God's love is present in all things. But why, Mr. Heschel, is Mr. Neibuhr not with us?"

"Please, Mary, call me Abraham, for I like the informality of this group. I suspect that the fundamentalists had heard of his use of the term 'original sin' in the Gifford lectures, and from that, assuming he was one of them, ordered St. Peter to add his name to the list. When they learn that he also said that a literal understanding of Adam and The Fall is nonsense, and that there is a hidden Christ in other religious traditions, they will certainly eject him from their 'heaven.' I believe he will be with us shortly...and, here he is now. Welcome to our group, Reinie."

"Thank you, Abraham. I'm not a bit surprised to find you in this group, for as I often said, you and others of different religious traditions often honor and love God and all of creation more than some who claim to be Christian. Some of those with whom I've been recently think they had achieved perfection because they are 'washed in the blood,' and, deluding themselves, do not acknowledge that when alive on earth they were as imperfect as are all human beings. Their self-righteousness is absolutely appalling. They chided me for opposing Mr. Nixon and the Vietnam War."

"Mr. Neibuhr, I'm Mary Cooley. My husband and I supported you in opposing the Vietnam War, but, holding to nonviolence as does Mahatma, I could not agree with your stance about entering World War II, as much as I grieved over Hitler's victims. My husband agreed with your position, feeling that Hitler and the Nazis must be stopped, but he was also aware of the fact that you took this position with a heavy heart, claiming that we need to acknowledge the sins of our own nation."

"Please, call me Reinie, as did Abraham."

"I will, Reinie, if you will call me Mary."

"Your husband was correct, Mary, about the heavy heart, for I felt that we should recognize the common humanity which binds us to even the most terrible foes of our common need for grace and forgiveness, and that, in addition, we needed to have a sense of pity for the victims of the struggle, whether ally or enemy."

"I am not surprised to see Jesus here associating with you and the others in this group, for his love, like God's, is for all of humankind and the world of nature. He wishes to persuade all, even those committed to struggling for power, to hatred, immorality, and acts of violence to accept the unsurpassable love of God that rejects power struggles, and seeks to replace hatred, immorality and violence with love. And I suspect, Jesus, that you've been doing just that in the other section of hell."

"That is very true, Reinie. It is a difficult task, for, as you know, love can be genuine only if it is freely given. It cannot be forced. So we must use persuasion, which means that the actualization of God's ultimate goal of a universal kingdom of perfect freedom, faithfulness, and peace of all humankind and the world of nature can take a very long time. But, Reinie, your 'Christian Realism' was certainly a step in the right direction. I especially liked your emphasis on love; that no act is quite as virtuous from the standpoint of foe or friend as it is from one's own standpoint, and thus the need for the final form of love which is forgiveness. Indeed, as Mahatma has said, 'An eye for an eye and whole world will go blind, and to befriend the one who regards himself as your enemy is the quintessence of religion.' So God's unsurpassable suffering love and desire to forgive is the message I'm delivering to the other section. It is a long, hard road, but I must keep at it. But before I go, I see that Siddhartha Guatama, the Buddha, has joined us. Welcome to our group, Buddha. I think we could profit from sharing a bit about our religious views."

"Thank you, Jesus. But call me Siddhartha instead of by my title, Buddha, as I have called you Jesus instead of using your title, Christ. I am pleased to meet you, Jesus, for I suspect that in spite of some important differences, there are also some very important similarities. From what I've heard here I know that both of us have emphasized a very radical kind of love for all, even for those who abuse us, and for all the animals, plants, and earth. I encouraged my followers to cultivate love without measure toward all beings and the whole world. If accused and attacked one should repress resentment and preserve a loving mind with no secret spite. **'For hatred does not cease by hatred at any time; hatred ceases by love—this is an old rule."** (Noss, *Man's Religion,* p.123) So, Jesus, while our ethical views are similar, they, as you know, have very different foundations in our theological perspectives."

"That is true, Siddhartha. I, too, emphasized the rejection of retaliation, mercy, love of enemies, meekness, peacemaking, and purity of heart, but the foundation for following this way of life is the acceptance of the unsurpassable love of a loving God. If I understand your four noble truths and eightfold path, this ethical way of life is self-attained through the elimination of wrong desire and strict self-discipline. I do admire the extensive discipline of you and your devout followers, but cannot agree that this must involve the rejection of a transcendent and spiritual eternal God of unsurpassable love, the acceptance of the law of Karma and belief in rebirth. Yet we do agree on that which, if fully accepted by humankind, would bring peace to the world. Unfortunately, our followers are not always faithful in living by our teachings. But now I must get back to those whom I am attempting to persuade to accept love, but I'm sure you will find a congenial group here, Siddhartha."

"Yes, Jesus, I'm sure I will, for it is rather obvious that everyone is convinced that the worth of human beings is not composed of knowledge, wealth, or skill, but in the acceptance and practice of radical love."

"Welcome to our group, Siddhartha. I'm Mahatma, who, as you, worked for the elimination of the caste system in our native India and for nonviolence and peace. Throughout my life I sought to find the good in all religions, and indeed, you and I have much in common."

"From what I've heard so far, Mahatma, that is certainly the case. For centuries I've been in a kind of No Man's Land, not knowing where I was, but most certainly not reborn into an earthly state of existence, and so I'm very happy to become a part of your group, the members of which are so accepting and loving. I am certainly willing to accept and be friends with those who do not agree with me concerning the issue of theism. And here comes another staunch believer in a radical theism, Mohammed. Welcome to our group, Mohammed. I know you brought about a great reform among the tribes on the Arabian Peninsula during your ministry. While I do not agree with a good deal of your theology, much of what you taught concerning morality and human relationships is similar to what is taught in many religions."

"I'm glad to hear you say that, Siddhartha, for there was much conflict in my homeland during my earlier ministry. In my many visions and messages from Allah it was made very clear to me that the primitive polytheism and animism, the widespread immorality, drinking, gambling, live burial of unwanted infant daughters, and lack of social justice for the poor present in the Arabian religion and society had to be opposed. I regret the warring factions had to be subdued by force. Also Islam often spread by military conquest. Yet there was generally a good deal of reform in common life and society."

"Prophet Mohammed, I'm Mary Cooley. I must say that I appreciate your reforms, but I do not appreciate the position of women in Islam or the spread of your faith by warfare. Of course, Christians cannot feel superior on this issue, since Christianity has spawned many wars. During my life on earth, as a pacifist I was distressed by war at any time and anywhere and wished that everyone would work hard for a peaceful world. I still wish that for the overpopulated world of today. I must say further that you should be proud of the great poets of the Sufi tradition, such as Rumi and Hafiz, for they were so close to God and God's creation. As Rumi said, **"If you put your heart against the earth with me, in serving every creature, our Beloved will enter you from our sacred realm and we will be, we will be so happy."** (Rumi, *Love Poems from God,* p.66) In addition, I remember from my college studies in world history how amazed I was at the notable developments in Moslem culture of the Middle Ages, such as the great universities where the works of the ancient Greek philosophers were studied and preserved and the hospitals where contagious sick people were isolated from other patients, the circulation of the blood was known and acknowledged, and transfusions given when needed. It is regrettable that such culture was of so short a duration, largely because of war. Don't you agree, Mahatma?"

"I could not agree with you more, Mary. Also, it is sad that in the three major theistic religions, Judaism, Christianity, and Islam, sometimes the concern for protection or expansion or domination led to actions that were in direct contradiction to the basic understanding of the nature of God and His relationship with the world as clearly and often vigorously expressed by some of the leaders and some of the scriptures. It is most certainly the case, as Dr. Heschel, Abraham, has expressed so beautifully in his writings, that God's compassion is at the core of Judaism. Then in Christianity there is, at the heart of the story about Jesus, a crystal clear and powerful emphasis on his compassion for others. And in Islam there is an insistence that Allah is the compassionate and merciful One. Indeed, every chapter of the Qur'an (114) begins with **"In the name of Allah the compassionate and merciful."** (*Fountain Magazine,* September-October issue, THE LIGHT, INC., publisher, Clifton, NJ, p.19) What do you think of those perspectives, Mary?"

"Oh, Mahatma, I think that it should open our minds and hearts to the beauty and goodness that can be found in the great religions of the world. I recall that when I was a student on earth, one of my favorite courses was World Religions. Somewhere in that course, one of the scholars said, at the conclusion of his book, that in all traditions there is both a high religion and a low religion, and that the adherents of all traditions should support the high religion as strongly as possible. Do you agree with that statement, Mohammed?"

"Yes, I do appreciate what you had to say, Mary. There is much in all of our traditions of which we can and should be ashamed and sorrowful. Surely, it was our obligation to God and humanity to abolish the shameful and to work as hard as we could to actualize that which is for the good of all humankind, namely, the unsurpassable love of God."

"Oh, Mohammed, I'm so grateful for your emphasis on love. Wouldn't it be great if all of humankind now on earth in the various religious traditions could learn to have a similar spirit of fellowship and love which we have in the post-mortem state of being."

ONE MORE STORY

One year at Yale Divinity School I was home for the summer and my father needed my help. Though by that point he was semi-retired and did not still have his own pastorate, my father continued to make the rounds as a circuit preacher, ministering to small communities and rural churches around Western North Carolina. He was good at it, and so was in demand. One Sunday he had double-booked himself for two churches in two separate towns and was in a bind. Though I hadn't technically finished divinity school yet, I was well on my way, and was a PK to boot. Dad asked for my help.

Sunday preaching was an all-day affair. There was the morning service. There was the receiving line after church. There was visiting with and counseling congregants. Then, usually, there was a break when the minister can rest, sleep, eat, and plan for the night. In the evening, there was another service to perform. In a town away from home a family usually arranged to house the itinerant preacher for the afternoon hours, and let him get at least a little rest. My father, when he was in that particular town, always spent the day with one particular kindly, devout, elderly woman in the congregation.

After my morning service, I was standing in the receiving line, garnering thanks and praise from the congregation (though I doubt it was deserved). People would walk up, introduce themselves, shake my hand, and say a little something. In what was perhaps my largest act of self-control, I managed to keep my composure in the next few minutes. In the middle of the line, a stately older woman approached and shook my hand, praising my sermon. She went on to say, "By the way, I am the woman with whom your father has been sleeping when he's in town." My God, I wanted to laugh. In retrospect I can't believe that I didn't. She was unaware of the sexual double entendre and I wasn't about to clue her in. Still, I could hardly wait until my dad picked me up that night to tell him what she'd said. On the way home, I told him and we laughed for a while. As the laughter was beginning to subside, he then turned to me, half-serious, half-joking, and said, "Son, if I were you, I wouldn't tell your mother about that one."

And I didn't.